T0360518

Japanese Management

Market Entry, Crisis and Corporate Growth

Japanese Management

Market Entry, Crisis and Corporate Growth

editor

Parissa Haghirian

Sophia University, Japan

 **World Scientific**

NEW JERSEY · LONDON · SINGAPORE · BEIJING · SHANGHAI · HONG KONG · TAIPEI · CHENNAI · TOKYO

Published by

World Scientific Publishing Co. Pte. Ltd.

5 Toh Tuck Link, Singapore 596224

USA office: 27 Warren Street, Suite 401-402, Hackensack, NJ 07601

UK office: 57 Shelton Street, Covent Garden, London WC2H 9HE

Library of Congress Cataloging-in-Publication Data

Names: Haghirian, Parissa, 1970–   editor.

Title: Japanese management : market entry, crisis and corporate growth / editor,
    Parissa Haghirian, Sophia University, Japan.

Description: New Jersey : World Scientific, [2021] | Includes bibliographical references and index.

Identifiers: LCCN 2020051964 | ISBN 9789811231025 (hardcover) |
    ISBN 9789811231032 (ebook) | ISBN 9789811231049 (ebook other)

Subjects: LCSH: Management--Japan--Case studies. |
    International business enterprises--Japan--Management--Case suties.

Classification: LCC HD70.J3 J39427 2021 | DDC 658.00952--dc23

LC record available at https://lccn.loc.gov/2020051964

British Library Cataloguing-in-Publication Data

A catalogue record for this book is available from the British Library.

Copyright © 2021 by World Scientific Publishing Co. Pte. Ltd.

All rights reserved. This book, or parts thereof, may not be reproduced in any form or by any means, electronic or mechanical, including photocopying, recording or any information storage and retrieval system now known or to be invented, without written permission from the publisher.

For photocopying of material in this volume, please pay a copying fee through the Copyright Clearance Center, Inc., 222 Rosewood Drive, Danvers, MA 01923, USA. In this case permission to photocopy is not required from the publisher.

For any available supplementary material, please visit
https://www.worldscientific.com/worldscibooks/10.1142/12124#t=suppl

Desk Editors: Aanand Jayaraman/Sandhya Venkatesh

Typeset by Stallion Press
Email: enquiries@stallionpress.com

Printed in Singapore

© 2021 World Scientific Publishing Company

https://doi.org/10.1142/9789811231032_fmatter

About the Editor

Parissa Haghirian is Professor of International Management at Sophia University in Tokyo, Japan. She has lived and worked in Japan since 2004 and is an internationally renowned expert in international management practices with a focus on Japan. Professor Haghirian earned an M.A. in Japanese Studies from the University of Vienna in 1999 followed by an M.A. and a Ph.D. in Business Administration from the Vienna University of Economics and Business Administration in 2000 and 2003, respectively.

In addition to her work at Sophia University, Professor Haghirian has been a visiting professor at HEC Paris, Keio University (Japan), Waseda University (Japan), Aalto University (Finland) and the University of Vienna. She held a professorship in Japanese Management at Ludwig Maximilian University (LMU) in Munich from 2011 to 2012.

Professor Haghirian has published numerous books, academic papers and articles on the topic of Japanese management. She is the author of *Understanding Japanese Management Practices* (Business Expert Press, 2010) and *Successful Cross-cultural Management: A Guide for International Managers* (Business Expert Press 2011), and she is also the editor of *Japanese Consumer Dynamics* (Palgrave Macmillan, 2011) and *The Routledge Handbook of Japanese Business and Management* (Routledge, 2016).

In addition to academics and research, Professor Haghirian advises major multinational companies on intercultural understanding and cooperation, and she coaches top global managers for success when working across cultures by providing new perspectives and skills. Professor Haghirian is a regular keynote speaker at conferences and corporate events in Europe, Japan and Asia.

www.haghirian.com

© 2021 World Scientific Publishing Company
https://doi.org/10.1142/9789811231032_fmatter

About the Contributors

Pavel Burak is a Master's candidate at Sophia University, Tokyo, studying in the Department of Global Studies within the subsection of Business and Development. He completed his undergraduate studies at Royal Holloway University of London in Accountancy, Finance and Economics. He also did internships in EY (London) and Alfa Bank (Moscow) where he focused on analyzing stock and commodities markets using fundamental and technical analysis.

Louis Chesneau is currently graduating from IESEG School of Management, Paris, France, where he will receive a Master's degree in Management with specialization in Finance. To reinforce his academic background, Louis studied at the Tecnológico de Monterrey in Mexico for a year and then six months at Sophia University, Tokyo, as an exchange student. He is now writing his final thesis in Finance for which he conducted "An empirical comparison of portfolios obtained using the mean-variance and Kelly criteria".

Sven Colen is a Master of Science candidate in market-oriented management at the WFI-Ingolstadt School of Management (University), Germany. He holds a Bachelor's degree in Law and Business from the University of Augsburg, Germany. In addition, he studied international management as an exchange student at Sophia University, Japan, and at Keimyung University, South Korea. Mr. Colen gained professional expertise as a management consultant in strategic management, business transformation and change management in a variety of industries in Europe. Moreover, he is co-founder of start-ups in the education, training and coaching fields.

Martha Denis moved from El Salvador to Taiwan in 2008 to pursue language in undergraduate studies and earned her B.A. in Business Administration and International Business from Tamkang University, Taiwan, in 2013. She continued to live in Taipei for three more years, working in the IT industry, before moving to Tokyo in 2016 to continue her education. She holds an M.A. in International Business and Development Studies from Sophia University, and a Joint Diploma on Sustainability Science from the United Nations University (2018). She continues to live in Tokyo where she practices judo and works for an IT consulting firm.

Xu Dong graduated in 2018 from Xi'an International Studies University in China with the honors of distinguished graduating student and excellent graduation thesis. She holds a Bachelor of Arts in Business English and obtained a Certificate in Business Accounting from the Chartered Institute of Management Accountants during her undergraduate study. She is currently pursuing a Masters in International Business and Development at Sophia University in Japan.

Shiyun Gu holds a Bachelor's degree in International Business from I-SHOU University in Taiwan. During her undergraduate studies, she also obtained an academic minor of Finance Mathematics. She is currently pursuing her Masters in International Business and Development at Sophia University in Japan.

Isaac Kim holds a Bachelor of Foreign Applied Languages from Jean-Moulin University, France (2016). He has spent a year abroad in Japan (Yokohama National University) and is currently pursuing his Masters in International Business and Development at Sophia University in Japan. Besides his studies, he has co-authored a trilingual dictionary under the guidance of a professor, as well as two other Franco-Japanese practice books.

Moritz Lahme is a Master of Science candidate in the field of Business Administration at the WFI-Ingolstadt School of Management in Germany. He is majoring in Finance, Accounting, Controlling & Taxation (FACT), where he previously gained professional expertise working in Accounting and Consulting firms. Additionally, he holds a Bachelor's degree in Business Administration from the Catholic University of Eichstaett-Ingolstadt, and was an exchange student at Sophia University in Tokyo, Japan. During his Bachelor studies, Mr. Lahme also studied as an exchange student at Xiamen University in China.

Le Ha My holds a Bachelor's degree in Journalism and Communication from Vietnam National University, Ho Chi Minh City. She worked full time as a staff writer and reporter for a daily newspaper in Vietnam before coming to Sophia University (Tokyo, Japan) to pursue her Master's degree in International Business and Development Studies.

Valerie Olenberger received her Bachelor's degree in Business Administration in 2017 from the Berlin School of Economics and Law in Germany. Currently, she is pursuing her Master's degree in International Business Administration at the Europa University in Frankfurt (Oder). In 2019, she attended an exchange program at Sophia University in Japan where she was part of the Graduate program in Global Studies.

Pierre Pitel is graduating from a Master's degree in Auditing and Accounting from IÉSEG School of Management (Paris) in 2020. He studied for a year at Özyeğin University (Istanbul) during his undergraduate degree and a semester at Sophia University (Tokyo) as part of his Master's degree. He is currently writing his Master's thesis on the implementation of new performance management in the public sector in France.

Tiantuo Yang holds a Bachelor of Science degree in accounting from Weatherhead School of Management at Case Western Reserve University in Ohio, the United States. During his undergraduate studies, he conducted research on the entrepreneurial ecosystem of Beijing. He is currently pursuing his Master's degree in International Business and Development at Sophia University.

© 2021 World Scientific Publishing Company
https://doi.org/10.1142/9789811231032_fmatter

Contents

© 2021 World Scientific Publishing Company
https://doi.org/10.1142/9789811231032_fmatter

List of Figures

Case 8

Case 9

Case 10

Case 11

Case 12

Case 13

© 2021 World Scientific Publishing Company
https://doi.org/10.1142/9789811231032_fmatter

Introduction

Parissa Haghirian

When editing the final version of this book, COVID-19 hit the world and changed the business environment, not only of Japanese companies, dramatically. At the time of writing this book in 2019 and 2020, the biggest problem local and foreign companies in Japan were facing was demographic change. The aging of the Japanese society as well as the decline in the birth rate of recent years not only led to lower customer numbers but also a decrease in the number of workers available in the Japanese labor market. In 2015, the Japanese economy was in full employment; since then, the number of available workers has been steadily declining.

The unemployment rate ranges between 2.2% (women) and 2.6% (men) and was (at the end of 2019) the lowest in 30 years. A few months later, the Japanese economy is struggling, the Tokyo 2020 Olympic Games have been postponed and the Japanese companies are developing new strategies to grow and internationalize.

Despite the unprecedented changes and challenges Japanese businesses face in 2020, the topics in this book are still relevant for their survival and long-term growth. The cases presented discuss three main topics of international management: entering new and/or foreign markets, how to manage corporate growth and how to deal with crisis. The first case describes the market entry of French bio supermarket chain **BioCBon** into the Japanese market. BioCBon, a highly successful French food retailer, entered Japan in the form of a joint venture with the Japanese market leader AEON in 2017. The market entry was very successful.

In the meanwhile, the company has 12 outlets in Japan, and has developed a very special marketing approach, educating consumers and involving them in a special way with modern social media marketing campaigns. The case shows that even in a very saturated market, it is possible to increase market share with the right concept. The case shows the challenges of the Japanese retail market.

The second case in this book presents **Mercari**, a Japanese start-up that not only became Japan's most successful start-up of the past years but also changed Japanese consumers' ways of thinking and shopping.

Established in 2013 by serial entrepreneur Yamada Shintaro in Japan, Mercari grew quickly into the most downloaded app in Japan. The application allows users to take a picture with their smart phone of used items and products and present them online for sale with just a few mouse clicks. The app became an instant success. Forty million Japanese use the online application and have started to sell unused items via it. This is particularly interesting since Japan is a country in which secondhand products were not so popular and consumers prefer newly purchased products. Mercari did not only attract investors from all over the world but, within a few years, it also had a long-lasting effect on Japanese consumer behavior and how Japanese buyers deal with purchases. Mercari's success created a lot of interest among Japanese and foreign investors. In the year 2014, the start-up decided to enter the US market. But, the American market proved to be a lot more challenging than expected. Now, the United Kingdom is the next market on the way to Mercari's globalization.

The next case is not located in Japan, but shows the success of an Asian start-up. **Grab**, an Asian taxi transportation service founded in Malaysia, developed from a small local competitor to Uber into a multi-industry million-dollar business. In his case "Uber Versus Grab — Entering Asian Markets Successfully" Moritz Lahme tells the story of the two companies in the transportation sector and compares the companies Grab and Uber and their management activities in South East Asia. Both companies offer taxi transportation services via an app. Uber is considered the world market leader in this industry and the first start-up developing this business model, whereas Grab is a local player in various East Asian countries. The case describes the development of both companies and compares their corporate success in Southeast Asia. The case focuses on Grab, trying to show that a local company knowing its market well can outperform a bigger player.

Case number four in this book features one of the most famous Japanese companies, **Uniqlo,** and its attempts to grow its business in the US. Uniqlo is a branch of the Japanese company Fast Retailing, which also owns companies such as Princess Tam-Tam or "Comptoir des Cotonniers". It is a retail company founded in Hiroshima in 1984 under the name "Unique Clothing Warehouse" by Tadashi Yanai. The company grew quickly into one of the biggest apparel corporations in the world. In the early 2000s, Uniqlo expanded internationally and opened shops in France, the UK, Malaysia, the Philippines, China, Taiwan and the US among others. However, the brand awareness outside of Asia was too low for the number of stores Uniqlo planned to open. Twenty-one stores were opened in and around London, and three malls in New Jersey. These market entries were rather challenging for the firm; next to the lack of brand awareness, there are different customer tastes and sizes to deal with. Intensive competition in the US market presented a big hurdle as well. The case investigates these issues and helps students to identify and develop successful strategies to overcome these problems.

The final case in this section discusses a rather new phenomenon: digital payments in the Japanese market. Japanese people are reluctant to switch to cashless payment methods such as credit cards or third-party electronic payment services, because of their obsession with cash. However, despite people's reluctance toward cashless payments, there are indeed many choices available for e-payment services in Japan. LINE Pay, Rakuten Pay, WeChat Pay and Alipay are the most common e-payment companies and they all have a unique target customer base.

The company this case study focuses on is the new blood in E-payment business, **PayPay**, a joint venture of Yahoo Japan, SoftBank and Paytm (an Indian company). PayPay Corporation was founded in June 2018, at the time when WeChat Pay and Ali Pay had already taken over the e-payment service market for Chinese tourists and Yahoo Japan's rivals LINE and Rakuten had already established their e-payment services, LINE Pay and Rakuten Pay. PayPay is now aggressively trying to establish itself in the Japanese market. The main two targets are to get Japanese customers to use electronic payment tools and to fight off foreign competitors in the market. The case discusses the strategies and challenges in doing this.

The second section of this book discusses corporate growth of Japanese corporations. TOTO, Japan's and the world's largest toilet manufacturer, has been manufacturing bathroom ceramics for almost a century and is the undisputable market leader in Japan. The company introduced its star product, the Washlet, back in 1980 and its success made TOTO a household name in the industry.

Currently, it is estimated that over 36 million Washlets have been sold worldwide; however, in the beginning, TOTO struggled domestically and the first launch of the Washlet was a failure. The company was quick to adapt after listening to customer complaints and hesitations about the product. In order to grow the domestic market, the company relied on strategic partnerships, technological innovation and marketing strategies to generate interest in its products. With the aging population and reduced construction projects, TOTO's domestic focus has been on the remodeling industry and Research and Development (R&D) development of green technologies for bathrooms and other applications. The case describes the development of the firm and which strategies are needed to grow internationally.

Another major Japanese player is Nippon Telegraph and Telephone (**NTT**) Group, a Japanese Enterprise with a revenue of over 100 billion USD, a huge player in the information technology (IT) and telecommunication industry and an extremely interesting company worldwide. NTT is a classic Japanese *keiretsu* and has acquired very many corporations worldwide. Until now, NTT behaved like a typical Japanese conglomerate investing overseas and collecting many companies all over the world.

Now, there are attempts to restructure and establish an "Extreme Large Deal Organization" (ELDO) as an umbrella organization for all NTT Group companies in the Western world. This strategic and structural bundling of the subsidiaries was supposed to be the next big step in the growth strategy. The goal was to acquire "Extreme Large Deals" (ELDs) in the IT industry. Here, an ELD is defined as an IT outsourcing and consulting project with a volume bigger than a hundred million US Dollars. The scope of an ELD is usually very wide and requires a large variety of IT capabilities. By regularly acquiring some ELDs each year, the NTT Group would push into a new business dimension and would finally belong to the largest IT and technology companies worldwide. The case describes the challenges of this process. Structural, cultural and managerial challenges are discussed.

Another interesting firm dealing with growth challenges is **Valve**, a digital distribution platform that initially only developed computer video game software. The first product "Half-Life" turned out to be a massive commercial success, something extremely rare for a debut product. Capitalizing on the initial impetus, Valve continued to release hit after hit for the next eight or so years. It was in 2003 that it finally developed Steam, first described as a digital software distribution platform integrating most of its previous works for self-promotion and ease of access. Steam attracted an estimated 18.5 million concurrent users in 2018. The company's main competitor is Epic Games. In December 2018, Epic Games announced its own Epic Games Store, a digital distribution platform similar to that of Steam. Epic Games promises hefty sums to developers signing their time-exclusive contracts. The case describes how market leader Valve deals with new competitors which aggressively access the market with innovative business models.

Another epic Japanese firm presented in this section is **Rakuten**, Japan's main competitor to Amazon. Rakuten, originally MDM Inc., was founded by Hiroshi Mikitani in February 1997 in Japan. At the time, it was the first and only e-commerce platform in Japan. Today, it is still the largest e-commerce website in Japan and the largest in term of sales around the world. Nevertheless, in Japan and in the world, it now faces fierce competition from other e-commerce websites like Amazon. The case describes the development of Rakuten, its business models and the ongoing and fierce battle with other players, such as Amazon in the Japanese and international markets.

In the third section of this book are cases dealing with corporate crisis and how Japanese companies deal with it. Here, we present one of the most prominent product scandals in the past years, the **Kao** Skin Care Scandal. In the early 2000s, Kao Group placed second on the market after Shiseido. In order to stay competitive, the Kao Group was on the lookout for expanding the business competitively. The area of cosmetics was of special interest since the market was constantly growing. In 2005, the cosmetics company Kanebo was listed for sale on the global market and the Kao Group saw a chance to acquire more cosmetics brands and to take the lead in the cosmetics industry. Kanebo was able to grow under the Kao Group and started to develop new products and formulas until, in July 2013, Kanebo was hit by a huge crisis again regarding one of its products. On the 4th of July, Kanebo recalled its first 54 products. Many users started to report symptoms of skin damage. Around 9000 people were affected, 2250 of them reported even serious damage. In the case crisis management, crisis publica relations (PR) is discussed.

Our next case is also located in the beauty industry and shows how **Shiseido Cosmetics** deals with the biggest company crisis in its history. Shiseido is one of the first cosmetics companies in Japan that advertised itself as a perfect combination of East and West. The company was also one of the first Japanese companies to expand abroad when it entered Southeast Asian markets as early as 1932 and started putting more emphasis on foreign markets in the 1970s. Ever since, the company has been enjoying its success as a global company with a great share of its revenue coming from outside Japan. In fact, currently, its revenue outside Japan accounts for 60% of the company's total revenue. Both the Japanese cosmetic market and the global market are equally important for the company. While the company has seen great success in the Asia Pacific region, both the European and US markets are still lagging. The case discusses the company's strategies to create a long-lasting competitive advantage.

Another famous Japanese company, **Sony,** is also struggling in one of its business fields. The case "Sony and the Gaming Business" by Pavel Burak analyzes how Game & Network Services (G&NS) has become the most profitable division for Sony in the past two decades. This sector in itself is a perfect example of vertical integration, since Sony produces hardware such as the consoles and also supplies this hardware with its own services and software, as well as making deals with outside publishers and occasionally acquiring them.

Not only is G&NS the best performing division of Sony Corporation but it has also become what Sony is known for, particularly with the younger generation. Most famous for Sony is the product PlayStation, not consumer electronics, which Sony was famous for until the 2000s. However, its electronics divisions, and especially mobile communications, have been generating losses over the past decade. The case discusses the development of Sony corporation, its business model and the how the company is trying to sustain competitiveness in very different industries at the same time.

The final case in this book, "Reviving a 200-year old Sake Business", describes the revival of a well-known Japanese business Asahi Shuzo in Hiroshima. The company, as a traditional sake brewery, has a 200-year history and was taken over by Sakurai Hiroshi. At that time, the business was facing strong competition and unprofitable structures. After the takeover, Mr. Sakurai restructured the business and focused on DASSAI, a high-quality sake that became one of the most famous Japanese sake brands internationally.

The case describes how a centuries-old business was revitalized and led into the 21st century and gives insight into traditional Japanese management processes and shows how they can be modernized and attract new customers.

This book still tries to show the variety of Japanese companies and their different interests and activities. It further attempts to help learners in business studies all over the world to understand Japanese management practices.

We hope that this book will increase the knowledge of Japanese companies and Japanese management practices.

Market Entry

© 2021 World Scientific Publishing Company
https://doi.org/10.1142/9789811231032_0001

Case 1

Bio c' Bon — The French Market Leader Entering the Japanese Food Retail Market

Parissa Haghirian

Organic Food on the Rise

The organic food market has become a very promising and growing segment of food retail in the past decades.

All over the world the organic food market is rapidly growing, about 15% or more per year. Leading markets are the United States and Germany. The biggest organic food market is the US with an average yearly sales volume of 28,9 billion euros. Germany follows with 9,5 billion euros and France with 6,7 billion euros (News European Parliament 2020; Organicnetwork, 2016). In Europe, the bio boom first targeted small groups of interested consumers, especially mothers looking for healthy food.

The organic food industry in Europe is a lucrative market, with the Western European market showing growth of 5.4% between 2015 and 2016. Germany is the leading market for organic products in Europe, with an 11.4% share of global organic sales, followed by France with 7.3% (Statista, 2020). However, other parts of the world are also catching up. Eastern European sales grew 8.8% in the same period (Statista, 2020).

Today — even though it took years for organically grown products to become widespread — they can be found in the discount food retail area in most European countries.

However, in Asian markets, organic food has also become more popular. Asian consumers are becoming more aware and concerned about agrochemicals in food products. This is also generating demand for organic products. The largest market in Asia is China, which has been showing a spike in demand for organic products for the last 10–15 years, while other important markets for organic products are Japan, South Korea, India and Taiwan. Here, the growth rates are about 15% per annum (Asia Pacific Food Industry 2019).

Bio c' Bon — The Company

A leading player in providing organic food to European consumers is the retail chain Bio c' Bon SAS in France. Bio c' Bon SAS was established in 2008 and until now has opened more than 140 organic supermarkets in France, half of them in Paris, which offer fresh perishables and reasonably priced products (Organicnetwork, 2016).

Since its start, the company expanded very quickly in France. After opening the first store in 2008, three more were opened in 2009, up to the record of 30 openings in 2015. In 2018, the company operated 123 stores and employed 1400 people (Daboval, 2019).

The company grew quickly not only in France but also expanded into other European countries such Italy, Spain, Belgium and Switzerland. Bio c' Bon SAS was so successful in this that corporate growth was organic as well; the brand took the risk to grow on its own, without acquisition and without outside investors (Daboval, 2019).

Expansion to Asia

The company's overseas expansion did not stop in Europe. Organic food is becoming a worldwide trend. The market is growing rapidly, also attracting "traditional" food retail corporations into the field.

In 2015, AEON, the largest Asian retailer and Japan's single-largest shopping mall developer and operator, expressed interest in a franchise system in Japan. Bio c' Bon SAS thought that due to specificities of the organic market, a development in Japan could only work if the mother company was invested in the project and so proposed a joint venture. BCB SAS established a 50/50 joint venture with AEON, called Bio c' Bon Japon (BCB Japon).

At the same time, AEON also proposed a franchise project to another French company, Picard, known for its frozen products.

The Japanese Organic Food market

The interest in organically grown products is not quite as great in Japan as in Europe.

Food Retail Market Players in Japan

Even if AEON is the major player in the Asian retail market, there are several reasons why AEON is looking for new business areas to expand into. The Japanese retail market is dominated by a few big players. AEON is the market leader and is known for experiments in the Japanese market. AEON is the first company to launch nationwide discount markets in Japan (*mai basketo*). AEON's own private brand, TOPVALU, is the best-selling branded product in Japan.

But, the Japanese market is also a challenge for AEON. Japanese retail companies are very successful but have a growth problem. Japan is a fully saturated market. Growth within Japan is hardly possible anymore. Japan's population is shrinking, as is the number of its consumers. Therefore, it is very difficult to increase market share and grow as a company. The Japanese retail market is therefore hotly contested. Supermarkets are no exception. Japanese providers are also specialized in taking a very close look at even the smallest customer groups and creating tailor-made offers for them. Every niche in the Japanese consumer market is served adequately and the struggle for each percentage of the market share is tough. Supermarket consumers are no exception.

One way to secure growth is to expand into other markets. Many Japanese companies are very successful in other Asian markets, such as China and Thailand. AEON has taken this route, as many Japanese companies have before.

Another Japanese phenomenon is the import of ideas from abroad. This Japanese tradition has been cultivated for hundreds of years. Rice cultivation was imported from Asia centuries ago and perfected in Japan.

Parts of the Japanese script are also imported from China and have been successfully integrated into the Japanese language. Japanese companies take advantage of this preference and are very interested in trends and changes abroad.

The organic boom in Europe therefore did not pass them by. Looking for new business opportunities, organic food retailing proved to be a promising market to enter. The company had some experience in the field; it was the first retail firm to offer organic products (Organicnetwork, 2016). This proved a great competitive advantage in setting up a supply chain for organic food in Japan.

Bio c' Bon JAPON

Bio c' Bon Japon entered the Japanese market in 2016. The plan was to make delicious bio products conveniently accessible (Foodex, 2019) with so-called "casual organic" stores.

To succeed in the highly competitive and sophisticated Japanese retail market, it was relevant to find a manager with a high degree of intercultural understanding of the Japanese market, who could not only manage expectations of both these, but could also be a bridge between France/Europe and Japan. Another relevant aspect is the relationship with internal and external stakeholders, notably local suppliers.

To manage the market entry, Bio c' Bon SAS hired a very talented manager, Pascal Gerbert-Gaillard, who speaks French and Japanese and had already worked for more than a decade in Asian markets. Pascal became not only manager of Bio c' Bon Japon but also the brand ambassador of the Bio c' Bon brand in Japan and Asia.

To have a French manager to co-run the Japanese business has many advantages. First of all, Bio c' Bon is a French brand. Having it represented by a French manager is a strong sign of authenticity for Japanese stakeholders. It was relevant for Bio c' Bon SAS to protect the overall idea of the brand while at the same time allowing for the required evolution in the business model and products to adapt to the local market needs. As a non-Japanese, Pascal was also able to push for more risk taking/experimentation/thinking out of the box to avoid falling back into the status quo Japan business-as-usual practices. At the same time, he can successfully protect and develop the French DNA of the business, explaining the difference in quality culture, how to market the products and adapt if required.

The company has a clear goal in the Japanese consumer market. "We offer 'casual organic' where customers would say 'this is where you'll find the best choices', but our goal for the future is to provide an environment in which people can fully transition their current lifestyles over to organic" says the CEO.

Organic products come from ingredients that innately have deep and strong flavors, and if we can convey the message of their good quality and taste, people will come to us of their own accord. As we work toward being the leading company in the organic field, "we want to increase numbers of organic consumers while becoming the center of topic, and to work together with producers to expand the supply of products" (Foodex, 2019), says Pascal in an interview about the firm's objectives in Japan.

Organic Farming in Japan

The greatest challenge in Japan turned out to be the search for organic products. Although Japan sees itself as an agricultural country, and AEON was the strongest partner in the retail sector, the awareness of or knowledge about organic products in Japan is neither well developed, nor is there widespread cultivation of organic products. In Japan, certification of organic products is still in its infancy. There is a division of the Japanese Ministry of Finance for healthy products, but this is not a certification in the European sense. Since 1999, the Ministry of Agriculture, Forestry and Fisheries developed a basic "Organic JAS Standard" and allowed certified businesses to use the "Organic JAS Mark" and the term "Organic Agricultural Products". This mainly referred to avoiding the use of chemically synthesized fertilizers and pesticides for more than a certain period prior while seeding or planting (MAFF, 2019).

Organic products have become increasingly popular in Japan in recent years. However, the Japanese agricultural structure is rather small and not very competitive.

In 2009, 16,000 hectares of farmland in Japan were used for organic farming. This number rose to 24,000 hectares in 2017. This may sound like a lot, but it still only accounts for 0.5% of the total farmland in Japan. And, even of these 24,000 hectares, only half were certified by the JAS standard. The rest was simply declared to be organic (MAFF, 2019).

However, the Japanese Ministry of Agriculture, Forestry and Fisheries has started different activities to support organic farming in Japan. One idea is to develop hubs of organic farming all over the country to establish the organic producers' networks, facilitate promotion to agricultural products buyer and consumers, and set up training farms for new farmers (MAFF, 2019). Still, these initiatives are small attempts to change the current focus on traditional farming using a high amount of pesticides.

In Europe, 10 million hectares were farmed organically in 2012. This number rose to almost 12 million hectares in 2016. In Austria, 21.3% of farmland is use for organic farming (News European Parliament, 2020).

In Japan, however, farming is an ailing industry. Many of the farmers are competitive only through subsidies and only manage small areas. Nevertheless, Japanese consumers are convinced of the high quality of the food produced in Japan. Even disasters like the tsunami in 2011 could not change this attitude. The problems of the farmers in Fukushima are seen as an exception, and food produced in Japan is generally seen as safer and healthier than food produced overseas.

Finding Organic Suppliers in Japan

It was a challenge to find the right providers for Bio c' Bon Japon. A major problem is the definition of "organic" in Japan. The Japanese ministry of Agriculture, Forestry and Fisheries developed the so-called JAS standard in the year 2000 for organic plants and organic processed foods of plant origin. Companies producing organic food can get certified and then receive the JAS standard and use the logo on their products. The logo can only be applied by registered business entities that have been certified by the registered certification body to verify that organic foods are produced in compliance with JAS (MAFF, 2020).

However, for many suppliers of food in Japan, this certification process is too complicated. In addition, many Japanese organic farms are often very small; they produce organic food, but do not find it necessary to get certified, since they only sell in their local community. In many cases, these small farms are not organized by wholesalers, which means they do not have access to supermarkets and cannot sell their products outside their own villages or provinces.

But, the fragmented structure of Japanese farming is not the only challenge. Of course, these farmers produce seasonally, which means they grow the products according to the season. For example, many suppliers offer cucumbers at the same time in June and another vegetable in September.

Japan is a very big country. Many farmers live and work far away from the big city centers. The small numbers of products they produce and the long distances (e.g. Hokkaido to Tokyo) increase the cost of logistics for BCB as well.

It proved a real challenge to find organic food. BCB was supported strongly by the Joint Venture partner AEON, but they still had to build a completely new logistic and sourcing structure for their Japanese business. BCB has more than 200 providers in Japan for fruits and vegetables, which are selected individually. In comparison, there are only five to six providers in France for the same category, mostly wholesalers, which makes processing easier and reduces costs.

Retail Channels in Japan

As mentioned above, the Japanese retail market is very competitive. But, it is also very complex. Many new store concepts are tested in Japan, every percentage of the market fiercely contested. Retail shops face serious competition, not only from other shops in the field but also from different store concepts.

A major field of competition in Japan is convenience stores, *conbini* in Japanese. Originally an American invention, convenience stores were introduced to Japan in the 1970s and started an unprecedented success story. Market leader 7–11 runs more than 20,000 stores in Japan and has successfully expanded all over Asia. Convenience stores in Japan differ from convenience stores in other countries. Convenience in Japan means helping busy Japanese customers improve their lives. A Japanese convenience store offers not only food and daily supplies but also offers postal services, dry cleaning, banking, payment and fax, it is also possible to eat in and get warm food. These stores are open 24 hours a day.

Another Japanese retail specialty is department stores or *depato*. Most Japanese department stores are managed via a shop-in-shop system. The most famous department stores in Japan are luxury department stores which offer a luxury shopping experience. Many famous luxury brands can be found in these stores. In the basement, there is usually a luxury food floor in which consumers can refresh, eat and buy delicacies. These floors are called *depachika* (department store basement stores) and have turned into a well-known tourist attraction as well. There is not a better place to taste and buy Japanese souvenirs and delicacies than in a *depachika*.

BCB Japon started to experiment with different store concepts in Japan very soon. "This is vital to be present and survive in the Japanese market," says Pascal. The company opened its first *depachika* in Ikebukuro in the basement of TOBU department store in November 2018 and its first convenience store in Jingumae station in August 2019. In these shops, products differ. The convenience store shopper prefers snacks and sweets, whereas the *depachika* targets well-to-do housewives interested in healthy organic food. As of February 2020, BCB Japon has one convenience store, three depachika stores and 10 classic supermarkets targeting everyday shoppers.

Japanese Consumer Behavior is Different

The Japanese consumer market is unique. Japanese consumers not only have a very high income but are also very experienced consumers, so-called prosumers. They are very concerned with their buying processes and carefully examine the products to be bought.

Particular attention is paid to the preference of Japanese products, especially in the food sector. Japanese food customers prefer fresh products. The reason for this is the preference for freshly cooked food and the small storage space in Japanese apartments. Japanese housewives therefore buy fresh food every day and cook freshly. This proved to be a challenge for foreign food retailers. BCB also wants fruits and vegetables to be as fresh as possible and in season, hence the effort put into sourcing local manufacturers and painstakingly getting supply from 200 suppliers.

This peculiarity has created many difficulties for foreign companies in Japan. French companies also learned their lesson here. The best-known example is Carrefour, the large French supermarket chain that opened a mega-store on the outskirts of Tokyo and had to leave the market after a few years. Here, too, the idea was that Japanese consumers would purchase a car-full of supplies during the weekend for their families. This failed because many Japanese families do not buy their groceries by car and — as I said — buy fresh every day.

Carrefour's failure in the Japanese market has left its mark. Many other companies have made their market entries in Japan much more carefully.

Another French player is Picard, a company specializing in Frozen Food. As explained above, the Japanese prefer to buy fresh food almost every day; frozen food is rather uncommon. Picard also entered the Japanese market with 12 shops, but the concept of selling frozen food is not convincing Japanese customers yet.

Organic Consumers in Japan?

Consumer attitudes

The fact that organic food did not have a long history in Japan was an advantage and disadvantage for the company at the same time. On the one hand, there are not yet very many rivals in the Japanese organic food market and BCB could establish a very strong impact in the market. On the other hand, Japanese consumers were not really familiar with the concept of organic food, nor how to use organic products. Even the term "organic" is not clear for many Japanese customers. In a survey by the Japanese Ministry of Agriculture, Forestry and Fisheries in 2018, 90.9% of Japanese Consumers reported that they know the term "organic", but only 3.7% were familiar with the correct definition of it. Nine percent of Japanese consumers had never heard of it, 86% of interviewees responded that they consider organic food as "safe", but 82.8% also considered it mainly as "expensive" (MAFF, 2019).

Community building

The fact that the concept of organic food is not so well known in Japan was a challenge for the company. Pascal and his team developed processes to support Japanese customers to learn about the relevance of organic food as well as how to use it in daily life. Bio c' Bon Japon started to run weekly workshops in their stores to provide education and spread the use of "fun, tasty, and healthy" bio products. As in Europe, organic food is entering into everyday eating habits very slowly. Many consumers are not familiar with organic products such as chia seeds or quinoa. To increase sales, educating consumers lowers entry barriers and allows customers to enjoy a variety of foods.

In France, this was done with vegetable and food bags, which came with a recipe. In Japan, food tasting proved to be a very successful measure too. Japanese consumers are very interested in foreign and gourmet food. To support them in learning more about organic food and cooking, special cooking seminars are offered. These seminars are very popular with young mothers and have successfully increased consumer interest in the products Bio c' Bon Japon offers.

Bio c' Bon Japon, being a supermarket, also offers a wide range of other products; next to fresh food, the shops sell other products too such as organic tea and cosmetics. This product mix, which is rather usual in Europe, was also introduced to Japanese consumers.

Social media campaign to attract and educate consumers

As of February 2020, 21,000 customers follow BCB on Instagram with a steady growth rate of more than 1000 new followers per month. This equates to 63% of Bio c' Bon France followers, with 10 times less stores after just three years in existence.

In Japan, attempts went even further. Here, online and offline marketing channels were used to attract consumers, educate them about the use of product and create a loyal community of buyers.

Bio c' Bon Japon offers cooking and information courses for their consumers, which are supported by social media campaigns. The company managed to successfully combine on-site and off-site communication. This was relevant, because there are a lot of products sold which are novel in Japan, such as Chia seed and Quinoa or many vegan products, and people do not know how to use them.

In France, store staff provide explanations, and many fruit or veggie bags are sold with recipes, but in Japan, a combination of online and on-site marketing activities supported the development and growth of a loyal customer base.

Impact in Japan and Successes

Within the first three years, the Bio c' Bon team could show a lot of successes, and efforts paid off. In 2019, Bio c' Bon Japon was elected Company of the Year of the French Chamber of Commerce in Japan.

They entered the market successfully and opened 14 stores in the highly competitive and saturated market, and they established two new shop formats for the company to adapt to market needs. The goal is 50 shops by 2022.

The concept of organic food is creating more and more interest among Japanese consumers. BCB stores in Japan show two-digit growth and more than 95% of customers are Japanese. The repeater levels (consumers who return to the shop) are similar to France. Also, the online media campaigns proved very successful. Bio c' Bon Japan already has 21,000 followers on Instagram, 63% more than Bio c' Bon France, and 1,000 new Japanese consumers follow the company every month. The company in Japan now has 400 employees, but not all are full-time; two managers in-store are full-time.

As mentioned above, the lack of producers in Japan was a serious challenge when entering the market. By increasing the number of stores, the company also managed to establish a stronger network with Japanese producers of organic food. Bio c' Bon Japon can now guarantee sales and show the suppliers a successful track record of store growth, which allows farmers and Bio c' Bon Japon to develop products together. The goals are a long-term partnership with local Japanese suppliers. However, these developments take time as do attitude changes.

Challenges Ahead

Since 2018, the cooperation with AEON became more intense. In December 2018, AEON bought a 19.9% stake of the French company. "They are not financing us, but are our business partners," said CEO Thierry Chouraqui (Daboval, 2019).

However, there are many challenges for BCB in the Japanese market. One major challenge is the labor shortage in the Japanese market. Japan is a country with a shrinking population. This has not only contributed to the shrinking number of consumers but also that of possible recruits.

The labor shortage in Japan is a dramatic problem for Japanese companies. In general, we can say that there are two open jobs for every job seeker. Japan's unemployment rate is the lowest in 30 years. This is good news for job seekers and university graduates, but a big problem for corporations. Every company is striving to get employee numbers to grow. However, the company members show a high dedication to the company and to the mission of making food supply in Japan more organic.

This can also be done by establishing more sales channels and supporting customers in having better access to organic products. Food delivery services are also a growing trend in Japan, but this can only be done if the number of suppliers of organic products can be increased.

Future Ideas

One important aspect of our customers in Europe is that they are buying organic out of a double concern: for their own health and for the environment. Hence, organic stores are at the forefront of waste reduction, banning plastic and non-reusable packaging.

The reduction of plastic used for packaging is another idea that has not yet become a concern for Japanese consumers. Even here, changes are visible. An increasing number of Japanese food retail stores (such as Fresco) are not handing out plastic bags anymore. Market giant AEON has introduced Topvalu, "My Bag" made from recycled materials. The bags (excluding the handles) are made from 50% recycled plastic and are on sale in all AEON stores all over Japan. The company has also started to sell environment-friendly products and to encourage customers to bring their own shopping bags when grocery shopping (AEON, 2019).

However, the idea of reducing plastic in stores and in packaging is still a big challenge. In Japan, the awareness of the need to reduce notably plastic usage is incredibly low, even though it is growing under foreign pressure (Olympics, 2020). Another important aspect is the decision of the Chinese government not to accept plastic waste anymore.

BCB decided not to offer plastic bags (selling instead paper bags and reusable cotton bags) and also introduced bulk sales for fruits and vegetables and for dry fruits and nuts in a dedicated corner. This strategy worked well with the dry fruits and nuts corner a success, but not with the fruits and vegetables.

Fruits and vegetables must be in plastic, an idea that most Japanese consumers agree with, because they think it is more hygienic. But, the overall goal is to become plastic-free in the next decade.

Questions

1. Which strategies did Bio c' Bon apply to enter the Japanese food retail market?
2. Why is so challenging for foreign companies to enter the Japanese retail market?
3. How did Bio c' Bon adapt its retail channels to the Japanese market?
4. How did the social media campaign support the success of Bio c' Bon in Japan?

5. Which strategies can Bio c' Bon develop to sustain longterm success in the Japanese market?

References

AEON (2019). Press Release May 23, 2019. Expanding the Lineup of Topvalu Environment-Friendly Products for Environmentally Conscious Shoppers (528KB). https://www.aeon.info/en/pressroom/. (Accessed March 5, 2020).

Asia Pacific Food Industry Online (2019). Asia leads growth for organic food market. https://apfoodonline.com/industry/asia-leads-growth-for-organic-food-market/. (Accessed February 24, 2020).

Daboval, A. (2019). L'ascension fulgurante de Bio c'Bon. Le Parisien.

Foodex (2019). Buyers Interview. https://www.jma.or.jp/foodex/en/img/trends/interview/japan_buyers_interview15.pdf. (Accessed on November 12, 2019).

Interview with Pascal Gerbert-Gaillard, October 15, 2019, Tokyo. BCB Japon.

MAFF (2019). Current situation and policy on organic agriculture in Japan. Sustainable Agriculture Division, Agricultural Production Bureau, MAFF (Ministry of Agriculture Forestry and Fishery). https://www.maff.go.jp/e/policies/env/sustainagri/attach/pdf/organicagri-1.pdf.

MAFF (2020). Organic JAS. MAFF (Ministry of Agriculture Forestry and Fishery). https://www.maff.go.jp/e/policies/standard/specific/organic_JAS. html. (Accessed May 9, 2020).

New European Parliament (2020). The EU's organic food market: facts and rules. https://www.europarl.europa.eu/news/en/headlines/society/20180404STO00909/the-eu-s-organic-food-market-facts-and-rules-infographic. (Accessed February 24, 2020).

Organicnetwork (2016). AEON and Bio c' Bon open new Organic Supermarket in Tokyo. https://organicnetwork.biz/aeon-and-bio-c-bon-open-new-organic-supermarket/. (Accessed on November 12, 2019).

Statista (2020). Organic food market in Europe — Statistics and Facts. https://www.statista.com/topics/3446/organic-food-market-in-europe/. (Accessed February 24, 2020).

© 2021 World Scientific Publishing Company
https://doi.org/10.1142/9789811231032_0002

Case 2

A Japanese Start-Up Conquering the World — Mercari

Parissa Haghirian

Entrepreneurship in Japan

Low rate of newly started businesses

Japan is not considered an entrepreneur-oriented country. This is rather surprising, considering the major Japanese corporations are successful today. After World War II, many young Japanese were eager to rebuild their country which had been completely destroyed by the war. Despite or because of this, enthusiastic entrepreneurs became the founders of many famous Japanese firms such as NTT, Honda and Sony (Cusumano, 2016). They started with great business ideas and were especially interested in manufacturing. Japanese firms started to produce high quality and reliable products and started to grow. The enormous success of their products all over the world allowed these companies to become very wealthy and to establish their unique management systems. Their focus lay mainly on stability and keeping their members inside the company dedicated and happy. Employees of Japanese firms started to enjoy lifetime employment practices; the companies preferred their members to stay their whole life in the same firm. They were very well trained and taken care of in these settings.

Until the end of the 20th century, Japanese companies grew enormously and became global conglomerates with a major influence in the world economy. Japanese employees enjoy a high degree of job security and many of them still prefer to work in the same firm all their lives. The success and reliability of the Japanese system is not only attracting Japanese nowadays but also an increasing number of foreigners to work and live in Japan and be hired locally by Japanese firms.

However, the Japanese corporate system has its price. Japanese companies are not only big and powerful but also provide a particular company environment. The majority of Japanese already work or prefer to work in these safe and reliable company settings. Even university students aim to enter a major corporation and start their careers in the classic Japanese system. This is not a surprise. Japanese firms not only offer lifetime employment, but also up to five months' bonus per year, health insurance and a pension plan. On top of this, many of these companies such as Mitsubishi Corporation, powerful like small economies, offer incredible career opportunities. Who would not prefer to start a career in an environment like this?

Despite these benefits, the safety and stability of the J-Firms have a negative effect on the intentions of Japanese to become entrepreneurs. Mostly new companies are founded by students who are aiming to become entrepreneurs while being in university. In the US, we have a number of famous examples (e.g. Mark Zuckerberg or the late Steve Jobs). In Japan, the attraction of getting a well-paid solid job in a big firm is often higher. The effect is that only 2.6% of university research was funded by companies, compared to 5.2% in the US (Munroe, 2017).

The second group of founders in OECD (Organisation for Economic Co-operation and Development) countries are mid-career managers who look for more independence and have enough experience to leave their firms after 20 years and start their own businesses (Haghirian, 2010). But in Japan these managers often prefer to stay on in their firms. They have invested many years of building relationships within the firms, they have often the opportunity to become top managers in their firms and are not very interested in taking the risk of founding their own firms instead. These long-term investments make it hard for start-ups to attract mid-level people (The Economist, 2016).

So even if Japan is still benefiting from the entrepreneurial spirit of its post-war managers, the number of high-tech start-ups in Japan is rather low. In 2014, the proportion of early-stage entrepreneurs in Japan was the second-lowest (Munroe, 2017). The scarcity of new firms is seen as one of the reasons for decades of slow economic growth (Cusumano, 2016).

Why is This a Problem?

So, what kind of companies are founded in Japan? Most of the newly founded businesses in Japan are low innovation businesses, founded in a local neighborhood, such as small bakeries, dry cleaning shops or local real estate offices. These businesses provide jobs for a handful of people and often play a very important role in local communities. However, they often lack modern business practices and the desire for growth (Haghirian, 2016). Many of these businesses exist for decades, but do not grow. Unlike in other OECD countries, such as the United States, the Japanese company owners are less inclined to dissolve existing firms probably for tax reasons (Cusumano, 2017). This means that existing firms are often not restructured or closed down, if business is not doing so well. But it is not a surprise that these small companies do not have a reviving effect on the Japanese economy. On top of this, the number of newly founded companies is still very low. Only 12% of Japan's small- and medium-sized firms are under five years old, whereas in the US the percentage is 33% (The Economist, 2016).

The low number of newly founded companies do not allow the economy to grow quickly. This is even more surprising considering the fact that Japan is a country with a strong ability to develop innovations and new products. One reason why it took so long to change people's and decision makers' minds about entrepreneurship is the fact that Japan has been a very successful manufacturing economy. After World War II, Japan became a leading country in manufacturing. High quality yet cost-effective processes allowed Japanese companies to become and remain the leaders in production and operations research. The leading firm in the field here is Toyota, which established the worldwide standard of JIT (Just-in-Time) manufacturing (Haghirian, 2014a). Japan and many Japanese still consider Japan as a manufacturing (*monotsukuri*) country and it took a while to realize that companies which do not operate a factory can still be very successful businesses.

Slow Changes and the New Role of Entrepreneurs in Japan

Over the past five years, attitudes towards entrepreneurs have slowly changed for the better. The interest in new businesses is increasing. In 2016, there were more than 200 business plan competitions in Japan

(Cusumano, 2017), mostly sponsored or supported by big Japanese conglomerates or companies. Famous entrepreneurs like Yanai Tadashi (Uniqlo), Son Masayoshi (Softbank) and Mikitani Hiroshi (Rakuten) dominate the news with their successful businesses and show that even modern Japanese entrepreneurs can found companies that become multinational giants within their lifetime. They have also changed the idea of entrepreneurship to being cool and successful. Also, the Japanese government has understood that change is needed. Prime Minister Abe has therefore pledged to make Japan "the world's most innovation-friendly country" and support Japanese businesses in developing technologies and innovation that will support economic growth (Munroe, 2017). This change in attitude is supported by success stories of young Japanese entrepreneurs who show that even in risk-averse Japan, new business models and start-up ideas can be successful and have the potential to become global players.

Yamada Shintaro and Mercari

Yamada Shintaro — An unusual entrepreneur

One of these young and enthusiastic entrepreneurs is Yamada Shintaro. He has a rather unusual biography. He studied mathematics at Waseda University, one of the best universities in Japan. Waseda is a very prestigious school whose graduates typically head to the country's top banks and blue-chip companies. He could have joined a big Japanese corporation to start a traditional Japanese career without problems. However, he preferred an internship developing an auction site for Rakuten Inc., at that time a little-known e-commerce site. During his internship he met Hiroshi Mikitani, now Japan's star entrepreneur, and saw how Rakuten developed into one of Japan's most successful internet corporations. It is now a retailing giant worth $14 billion. After graduation, Yamada founded his first firm, a company called Unoh (Japanese for right brain) in 2001. The company produced several hits and was acquired by Zynga Inc. in 2010 (Alpeyev and Amano, 2016).

After a long holiday, taking an around-the-world trip, Yamada Shintaro became interested in developing a firm based on mobile business. In 2013, the idea for Mercari, a flea market app, was born. The company was started with two other partners, Tommy Tomishima and Ryo Ishizuka (Mitra, 2016).

Starting Mercari

Mercari is a peer-to-peer (P2P) flea market app (Ng, 2018), called "*furima apuri*" in Japanese (see Figures 1 and 2). Mercari targets everyone who is interested in selling everyday items, such as clothes, CDs or baseball tickets. App users can take a picture of the item they would like to sell, upload it and offer it online within a few minutes. Mercari only charges a very low fee for its services so even products for a few dollars can easily be sold with a profit. This allows users to quickly sell items they do not need any more, even for only a few hundred yen. The company charges 10% of each sale it makes in Japan (Shu, 2016).

The app was a great success. When the app started in 2013, the Japanese internet market was dominated by Yahoo Auction (Ng, 2018). But the existing players were aiming at power sellers and seemed to be forgetting about the regular, casual sellers. Selling was too complicated for normal users. "To take on this market, we focused on smartphone users. Once we were successful in creating a great selling experience on smartphones, we saw very rapid growth," said Shintaro Yamada (Kamps, 2016) about the market niche he discovered. Nine million users signed up within 18 months; it allows everyone to sell non-used products within seconds. More than 1,00,000 of items are uploaded every day (Ng, 2018). This success was made possible by the changing ways in which consumers are buying their goods. More and more Japanese customers are using *furima apuri* apps to buy goods directly from other consumers (Meola, 2016).

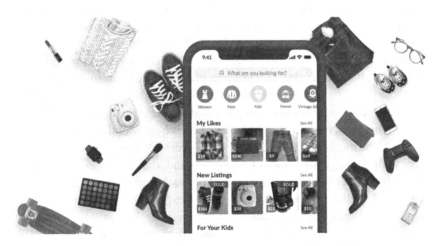

Figure 1.   Mercari advertisement (www.mercari.com, 2020).

Figure 2. Mercari logo (www.mercari.com (2020). www.mercari.com/jp/ Accessed November 11, 2020).

In 2016, the company achieved ¥13 billion ($127 Million) of revenues in Japan (Kamps, 2016). Secondhand sales are now a big business in Japan and a market worth ¥1.6 trillion (Alpeyev, 2017). This boom was supported by the start of Mercari. After only three years, the company now resides in Roppongi Hills next to Google and Goldman Sachs (Alpeyev and Amano, 2016).

Mercari's Success in Japan

Changing consumer attitudes

Secondhand products were not always so popular in Japan. During bubble times in the 1980s when Japan became one of the richest nations in the world, Japanese consumers discovered shopping and traveling as a leisure activity. Millions of Japanese went overseas to do sightseeing, but they also changed the Japanese consumer markets. Japanese companies, which — until the 1970s mainly produced for overseas markets — realized that Japanese consumers were not only wealthy enough to shop for consumer goods, but they were also increasingly interested in high quality and high technology products. On top of this, their taste was very Japanese and they responded well to products that represented Japanese quality. During bubble times, a high price was synonymous with high quality and Japan gained the image of the most expensive country in the world. Japanese consumers were very willing to pay high prices for products and to dispose them quickly for better and newer versions. Buying used products was unheard of.

In 1990, the bubble burst and Japan experienced a long economic depression. Many Japanese consumers changed their consumption behavior. They became more cost-conscious and spent less (Haghirian, 2014b). Companies like Uniqlo picked up this trend and produced high quality and yet affordable products, which became an instant success.

New business models were introduced to Japan. eBay tried to enter the Japanese market but was outperformed by its Japanese competitor Yahoo Auction. Yahoo Auction was the first internet company to allow consumers to sell and buy to and from each other and is still the market leader in Japan. However, it mainly targets a middle-class audience. It focusses on higher priced products and allows consumers to sell art, antiques and even real estate. Yahoo Auction also charges a rather high fee, so selling cheap items was not profitable for its users. Mercari's new app was introduced at the right time. The company did not try to be another Yahoo Auction, but offered a service for a segment that was not adequately served by other Japanese online businesses. It made it easy for young smartphone users who have extra stuff to sell it for a quick buck (Ng, 2018).

The app's easy usability also affected Japan's attitude towards used products. Everything can be bought and sold easily with a few mouse clicks. Young people especially find the app easy to use. One wonders if the attitude of Japanese consumers towards secondhand products has changed quickly or whether the easy usability of the app made it so popular. Probably it was time for the right app.

Japanese Delivery Services Supported the Business Model

Mercari's app was supported by some particularities of the Japanese market, e.g. Japanese delivery services. Every product can be delivered to any address in the country — parcels, luggage, art items, bottles and even frozen food. The items to be delivered can be posted from every convenience store in Japan or will be picked up right from people's houses. Delivery is cheap (average 1,700 Yen for a mid-sized parcel around the country) and takes a maximum of two days for a distance of more than 1,000 km — Japanese consumers are very used to convenient delivery. These services and their reliability support Mercari's business model. Mercari mainly targeted smartphone users (Ng, 2018) and this made the app extremely attractive for young Japanese users interested in selling cheaper items such as shoes or video games.

Sellers can send their products within minutes to their buyers, and buyers can have their purchased items delivered at exactly the right time. The company found a solution for this with their logistics partner, Yamato Holdings, that helps deliver the products (Corbin, 2016).

On top if this, Mercari uses a third-party payment service to hold payment or prevent fraud and any settlement issues. Sellers will only receive their payment after buyers have confirmed the receipt of the item. The payment service company will further settle any item disputes (NG, 2018). Another big obstacle for potential sellers in Japan is to go wrapping the sold item, ask for and write down buyer's address, pay shipment fee, and so on. Even this is taken care of by Yamato Holdings (Corbin, 2016).

Japanese consumers spend an average of 40 minutes per visit on the platform. They flip through it like a magazine looking at different items on sale (Shu, 2018). It does not take more than three minutes to list an item on the Mercari marketplace (Corbin, 2016). By the year 2017, the flea market app had been downloaded more than 40 million times in Japan (Kyodo, 2017), with 30% of the Japanese population using the platform to buy and sell new and used goods (Kamps, 2016). These are just some reasons for the success of the application. At Mercari, sale products in the women's category (women's clothing, bags and accessories) account for more than 25% of total sales (Sankei Biz, 2018). Fifty percent of the products presented online are sold within 24 hours (Sankei Biz, 2018) and one million items are posted every day (www.nhk.or.jp, 2017).

Japanese Seller and Buyer Ethics

Usually sellers would show not only a number of pictures of the items, but also explain very carefully whether the product has a stain or scratch. Buyers in Japan can rely on the honesty of the sellers. Return rates are therefore rather low. The company is strictly focusing on C2C business — professional merchants are not welcome at the application. A customer team of 100 people is supervising online activities (Shu, 2016).

Japan's Only Unicorn is Setting the Stage

The company raised 8.4 billion yen (about $75 million) at a valuation of over $1 billion by investors such as Mitsui & Co, Development Bank of Japan Inc., Sumitomo Mitsui Trust Bank's Japan Co-Invest and other overseas investors (Shu, 2018). Mercari therefore became the first Japanese start-up valued at more than $1 billion (Alpeyev, 2017). The Chief Financial Officer Kei Nagasawa of Mercari said that this funding would go towards expansion in Japan, the United States and Europe (Meola, 2016). This has made Mercari a so-called 'unicorn', Japan's only start-up unicorn.

But what is a start-up unicorn? The term unicorn refers to companies included in the so-called The Global Unicorn Club of private companies valued at more than $1 billion (Asia Nikkei, 2018). However, Mercari is the only Japanese unicorn so far and there are not many Japanese promising start-ups to follow in its steps (Sekiguchi, 2017). There are only 155 companies that classify as unicorns in the world (92 in the U.S., 25 in China and seven in India) (Alpeyev and Amano, 2016). Mercari is the only unicorn in Japan, a fact that has a strong effect on the attitude of investors and potential future entrepreneurs. Attitudes of potential entrepreneurs are changing. The Economist (2016) reports that already 19.5% of Japanese who believe they have the ability set up a firm are starting a business, while only 17.45% of Americans do so. Tokyo is becoming a new hub for Japanese and international entrepreneurs and start-ups — Mercari has broken the spell. But Mercari uses its success to grow. In 2017, the company bought its local competitor Zawatt, a social media application developer, and continued one of its products, Smaoku, where secondhand branded goods are sold (Gaung, 2017).

Mercari's Growth Strategy — Going International

After the incredible success, Mercari faced the same problems as many Japanese companies in the past decade. Which strategy should be developed now that the company is facing a saturated market? It found the same answer as most Japanese multinational corporations — it went overseas and decided to enter the US Market.

The company and its founders have always been clear about their goal to enter global markets. Their first choice was the United States. This came a bit of a surprise for many observers, since Japanese companies often enter other Asian markets when first going overseas. These markets show some similarities to the Japanese market and the interest in Japanese products or services is generally very high. Many investors expected Mercari to go down the same road and follow the footsteps of many other Japanese start-ups and head to Asia. But the company decided not to compete with local players like Carousell or Rakuten's new Taiwanese flea market app, called Rakuma (Corbin, 2016).

Instead, Mercari chose the United States, a bold choice considering the fact that it is the home market of internet and retail pioneers such as Amazon.com and eBay. "We really saw the US as a gateway to the rest of the world, to becoming a global company," said Ishizuka Ryo, the CEO of Mercari's American business unit (Moazed, 2016). Mercari's services have been available there since September 2014 (Alpeyev and Amano, 2016). Even if Mercari is moving away from traditional internet business and mainly focuses on mobile e-commerce, it faces challengers such as Wish, Jet and Poshmark (Meola, 2016). Some compromises had to be accepted. Mercari dropped the 10% transaction fee in the United States to gain fast access to the market. This strategy paid off; the app had been downloaded 7 million times until 2016. However, American users are less loyal than Japanese users (Alpeyev and Amano, 2016). Unlike Japanese, American users are looking for particular products when using the app; they browse less and spend less time using the application (Shu, 2016). And users are harder to retain. To gain more ground, Yamada has announced plans to use venture money to strengthen marketing activities via social media channels such as Facebook (Alpeyev and Amano, 2016).

Challenges of the United States Market

The US market differs greatly from the Japanese market, not that US consumers mind buying secondhand products. There is an existing secondhand market in the United States, but the infrastructure is not as well developed as in Japan. In Japan, Mercari partnered with delivery services such as USPS and FedEx for shipping the items and cooperates with Braintree as a payment vendor (Shu, 2016). However, delivery services in the United States are less reliable than in Japan.

Another challenge is differences in seller and buyer ethics. Mercari operations in the US suffer from 10 times more fraud than the Japanese unit (Kamps, 2016). Yamada Shintaro was very surprised by this: "We knew there would be a difference compared to Japan, but we were surprised by the volume of enquiries. Our customer service load in the US is a lot bigger than in Japan." he said in an interview (Kamps, 2018). To improve and keep customers' trust in the brand and app, the company Mercari refunds the transaction to the buyer who gets through the safeguards (Moazed, 2016).

However, even in the US the market reacted positively to the new flea market app. In November 2016, the company announced 20 million downloads in the US (Kamps, 2016) and 60 million downloads globally (Presswire, 2017). In 2016, its gross merchandise value exceeded $88 million per month (Meola, 2016).

The Next Step — The United Kingdom

Internationalization of Mercari did not stop in the United States. In 2017, the company entered the United Kingdom as its second international market (Presswire, 2017). Yamada Shintaro told the press: "We live in a world with limited resources, and our mission at Mercari is to eliminate waste and inspire reuse by creating value in a global marketplace where anyone can buy and sell. Truly passionate about this mission, we hope to reach as many people as possible by continuing to expand throughout Europe and the rest of the world, starting with the UK" (Presswire, 2017).

Into a Mobile Future

Mobile online retailing is on the rise and sales still aren't keeping up with retail traffic. Smartphone traffic is higher than traffic on tablets and desktops (53% of all online traffic). Despite this, mobiles still only accounted for 29% of all online sales. Many traditional retailers are still lagging behind in their mobile presence. Only 60% of the top 100 global retailers have currently developed a mobile website (Meola, 2016).

Using its experiences in the mobile business, the company just launched a new business, a mobile bike-sharing service in the southwestern Japanese city of Fukuoka. A fleet of 400 bicycles will be available and the company would like its users to use Mercari in the real world as well. And there were big hopes to expand the business to a bike fleet of 2,000 in 2018 and to expand the business gradually into other service areas (Asia Nikkei, 2018).

Undoubtedly, Mercari has very ambitious global plans in the mobile industry. But how will Mercari continue its growth process? The company said that it is also open to merger and acquisition possibilities (Meola, 2016), is still interested in expanding overseas and is open to foreign investors funding these dreams (Corbin, 2016). But further expansion will come with more challenges. Which further challenges will Mercari meet on its way to becoming a global company?

Questions

1. Why is the rise of Mercari in Japan so special?
2. What attitudes do Japanese consumers show towards secondhand products? How did this attitude change? How did Mercari influence this development?
3. What is a unicorn and why is Mercari the only unicorn in the Japanese market?
4. Which challenges does the company face in the American market?
5. Why did it choose the US market to internationalize?
6. How can Mercari increase its market share in the United States? Which strategies should it develop to deal with competitors?
7. The company has just entered the British market. Is Europe ready for Mercari?

References

Alpeyev, P. and Amano, T. (2016). How $5-a-night hostels led to Japan's first $1 billion startup. *Bloomberg.* (Accessed on March 18, 2016).

Alpeyev, P. (2017). 36-year-old strikes gold with instant web Japanese flea market. *Bloomberg.* December 4, 2017.

Asia Nikkei (2018). Japanese unicorn Mercari charging into bike-sharing; Flea market app operator pedals into the real world. February 14, 2018, https://asia.nikkei.com/Business/Companies/Japanese-unicorn-Mercari-charging-into-bike-sharing. (Accessed on March 13, 2018).

Corbin, D. (2016). Japan, you have a unicorn. Mercari's valuation rises over $1b. www.techinasia.com, March 2, 2016. https://www.techinasia.com/mercari-japan-unicorn. (Accessed on March 13, 2018).

Cusumano, A.M. (2016). The puzzle of japanese innovation and entrepreneurship. *Communications of the ACM*, Vol. 59, No. 10 (October 2016), pp. 18–20.

Gaung, J.S. (2017). Mercari, a Japanese unicorn e-commerce start-up buys local rival Zawatt, www.dealstreetasia.com, February 21, 2017. https://www.dealstreetasia.com/stories/mercari-a-japanese-unicorn-e-commerce-start-up-buys-local-rival-zawatt-65578/. (Accessed on March 13, 2018).

Haghirian, P. (2010). Understanding japanese business practices. World Scientific Publishing.

Haghirian, P. (2014a). Japanese economy and management. In: Babb, J. (Ed.) The Sage Encyclopedia of Japanese Studies. London: Sage Publications.

Haghirian, P. (2014b). Japanese consumers and consumerism. In: Babb, J. (Ed.) The Sage Encyclopedia of Japanese Studies. London: Sage Publications.

Haghirian, P. (2016). Entrepreneurship in Japan. In: The routledge handbook of japanese management and business. P. Haghirian (Ed.). Basingstoke: Routledge Publishing.

Kamps, H.J. (2016). Japanese unicorn Mercari is gunning for ebay's crown. Techcrunch.com, November 18, 2016. https://techcrunch.com/2016/11/18/watch-out-ebay-here-comes-mercari/. (Accessed on March 4, 2018).

Kyodo Staff Report (2017). Mercari e-commerce site bans listing of currency for sale. April 25, 2017, Online Version. (Accessed on February 2, 2018).

Meola, A. (2016). Shopping app Mercari becomes first Japanese unicorn. www.businessinsider.com, March 2, 2016. http://www.businessinsider.com/merc-ari-passes-1-billion-valuation-32-million-app-downloads-2016-3?IR=T. (Accessed on March 13, 2018).

Mitra, S. (2016). Billion dollar unicorns: Japan's mercari joins the club. Sramanamitra.com, May 24, 2016. https://www.sramanamitra.com/2016/05/24/billion-dollarunicorns-japans-mercari-joins-the-club/. (Accessed on March 5, 2018).

Moazed, A. (2016). Mercari doesn't think e-commerce is a done deal; Japanese unicorn and marketplace platform Mercari is making a huge global play and taking market share from the likes of Amazon and eBay. www.inc.com, December 21, 2016. https://www.inc.com/alex-moazed/mercari-sees-room-for-disruption-in-e-commerce.html. (Accessed on March 13, 2018).

Munroe, I. (2017). Dusting off outdated patterns. Nature Index 2017/Japan. MacMillan Publishing, pp. 24–26.

Ng, A. (2018). Mercari, the unicorn startup that took Japan by storm. Linkedin. https://www.linkedin.com/pulse/mercari-unicorn-startup-took-japan-storm-audrey-ng. (Accessed on March 4, 2018).

Presswire (2017). Japan's #1 marketplace app Mercari launches in the UK. Presswire, March 15, 2017. https://presswire.com/content/1148/japans-1-marketplace-app-mercari-launches-uk. (Accessed on March 6, 2018).

Sankei Biz (2018). *Mercari kōhō ni kiita ureru aitemu nesage kōshō saretara.* Sankei Biz, January 21, 2018.

Sekiguchi, K. (2017). After Mercari, where are Japan's unicorns? Japan, unlike US and China, lacks many IPO-ready startups. www.asianikkei.com, July 25, 2017. https://asia.nikkei.com/Markets/Tokyo-Market/After-Mercari-where-are-Japan-s-unicorns. (Accessed on March 13, 2018).

Shu, C. (2016). Marketplace app Mercari nabs $75M to become Japan's first startup unicorn. Techcrunch.com, March 1, 2016. https://techcrunch.com/2016/03/01/mercari-unicorn/.

The Economist (2016). Entrepreneurs in Japan. How to rev up Japanese startups. The Economist, Print Edition, November 5, 2016.

www.mercari.com (2020). www.mercari.com/jp/. (Accessed on November 11, 2020).

© 2021 World Scientific Publishing Company
https://doi.org/10.1142/9789811231032_0003

Case 3

Uniqlo in the US

Pierre Pitel

Tadashi Yanai

The story of Uniqlo began in Japan in 1949 when Hitoshi Yanai founded Ogori Shoji (which was rebranded as Fast Retailing in 1991), a men's clothing company producing high-quality formal wear for men. Tadashi Yanai, the son of Hitoshi Yanai, graduated from Waseda University in 1971, and joined his father's company to assume the position of Director of Ogori Shoji, taking over the 22 men's tailoring stores of the family company in 1972.

Tadashi Yanai, who would later assume the position of managing director of the company after his father retired in 1984, opened the first Uniqlo shop in Hiroshima under the name "Unique Clothing Warehouse", which would be shortened in the future. Inspired by his travels to Europe and the US, Tadashi Yanai observed the growth of the casual clothing market share through brands such as Gap and Benetton and decided to exploit this potential in Japan to contrast with the conformity of Japanese fashion habits. At this time, the Uniqlo brand did not exist as such and Uniqlo stores were selling private label products (Haghirian, 2014).

The objective of the store was to develop good-quality clothing at a low price and in a large array of colors for families. While the economic growth of the mid 1980s in Japan embodied the rise of more diversified and expensive brands, the standardization of Uniqlo stores and products aiming toward a broad consumer market allowed for a cost reduction which was reflected in the global price of clothing.

Following the collapse of the Japanese asset price bubble, the exchange rate of the yen depreciated from 225.40 to 260.24 against the dollar, a move of 14%. Uniqlo then needed to reduce their overall production costs to maintain the low prices that were particularly effective due to the Japanese consumers becoming price sensitive — buying clothes in Uniqlo was a way for households to cut down their expenses and led to the increase in its popularity (Obstfeld, 2009).

In 1987, Tadashi Yanai met with the representatives of Jelldarno in Hong Kong, a company that sold overseas in the United States and in Europe, to commission the factory behind Jelldarno products with the manufacturing of the Uniqlo brand. As Uniqlo began producing their own brand, the company was to operate as a manufacturer and a distributor. All the steps of creating a Uniqlo product were in-house, following an SPA strategy — Specialty store retailer of Private label Apparel. From the sourcing to research and development and in-store delivery, Uniqlo was to oversee all operations.

Once the Uniqlo brand was launched, Tadashi Yanai established a franchise system and reduced costs through economies of scale, especially on intemporal clothing provided by Uniqlo. As such, Uniqlo obtained control over the entire value chain and started their success story of being the first to provide casual clothes to Japan, where 50 stores opened in 1992. This number doubled by 1994 and rose to more than 300 in 1998. As a company, UNIQLO's message is as follows: "UNIQLO is a modern Japanese company that inspires the world to dress casual." In 1997, Uniqlo stores stopped selling other brands and focused only on their own production (Haghirian, 2014).

While every aspect from the thinking, production and delivery is overseen by Uniqlo, most operations do not operate in Japan anymore. Research and development are separated in two R&D centers, New York and Tokyo, where UNIQLO gathers information on different trends, local news, lifestyles and material. Then, a concept is determined for each season and the designs are created in each center and compiled to meet every target.

Procurement and production are essential to the retail industry. Ninety percent of UNIQLO products are manufactured in China in seventy companies which are overseen by UNIQLO through technical support and quality management, mainly in the Shanghai area, but also in Ho Chi

Minh City (Vietnam), Dhaka (Bangladesh), Jakarta (Indonesia) and Istanbul (Turkey). Due to the high number of worldwide UNIQLO stores, the company benefits from economies of scale and negotiates with textile manufacturers such as Toray Industries.

Technology and UNIQLO

The success of UNIQLO can be related to the product lines shown to the consumer. In 1994, UNIQLO released a fleece jacket that became trendy especially through the 1900-yen fleece campaign operated in 1998 to promote the garment, creating LifeWear, pieces of clothing not to be thrown away when the fashion trends move, but to be worn in the daily life with intemporal fashion (Figure 1).

While its competitors such as Inditex and H&M strive to follow the fashion trends, UNIQLO focus on providing simple but essential clothing while not neglecting the performance of its apparel. Contrary to Zara developing products in less than a month, the production of technical clothing at Uniqlo is usually planned a year in advance.

Figure 1. Flyer for the 1900-yen fleece campaign (www.uniqlo.com, 2020).

In 2004, the company released heat-generating technology for winter clothes to manufacture extremely lightweight products keeping a maximum of heat. This clothing line, HEATTECH, is renewed every winter.

In 2012, UNIQLO announced the launch of AIRism, its new brand of highly functional underwear as "Comfort unlimited, in any season, for any person, anywhere". Using their fiber technology, the underwear of the AIRism line includes both the DRY technology evacuating the moisture and sweat and eight enhancing features for extra comfort.

In 2018, UNIQLO released their BLOCKTECH jacket, a lightweight windproof and water-repellent jacket to protect the owner from heavy rains when the temperature is too high for a traditional coat, while not neglecting the urban style of the jacket. In 2019, UV Cut technology was developed to protect the consumer from UV radiations caused by the sun.

According to its president, Tadashi Yanai, "Uniqlo is not a fashion company, it's a technology company." With a focus on climate-adapted technical clothing, Uniqlo exceeds its competitors' brand awareness related to outerwear as it becomes known year after year that Uniqlo's clothing can be adapted to any situation.

Brand Identity and International Penetration

The first perception from the Japanese consumers on Uniqlo products and even the first stores in which other labels were sold were not unanimous. Uniqlo was initially seen as a discount retailer selling cheap, low-quality clothing, which is the opposite of the perception UNIQLO looked for prior to the economic crisis of 1985. It took the economic crisis and the opening of a three-story store in the fashion district of Tokyo, Harajuku, in 1998 for UNIQLO to be perceived as a high-quality brand.

In the early 2000s, Uniqlo expanded internationally and opened shops in France, the UK, Malaysia, the Philippines, China, Taiwan and the US among others. However, the brand awareness outside of Asia was too low for the number of stores Uniqlo planned to open. Twenty-one stores were opened in and around London and three malls in New Jersey. Within eighteen months, all stores in New Jersey and sixteen out of the twenty-one opened in London closed due to lack of customer interest.

After the failure of the expansion overseas in the early 2000s, Tadashi Yanai reviewed Uniqlo's strategy. He hired the Japanese designer Kashiwa Sato and asked him to organize the creative resurrection of Uniqlo for the international market. Sato told Yanai that everything had to be redone since Uniqlo was considered uncool; otherwise, there would be no chance to implement the brand in places like New York, London or European cities.

The turning point in Uniqlo's brand awareness was the collaboration with the German designer Jil Sander, "+J". Jil Sander was a big name in the minimalist fashion industry and retired shortly before this collaboration. The collaboration was especially important in New York, at the flagship Uniqlo store in SoHo. Customers were lined for blocks, waiting hours to obtain some items from the collection.

This collaboration strategy had been popularized by H&M and adopted by Uniqlo: there is a high positive return from customers when it comes to low-cost brands working with fashion designers usually associated with luxury brands. Therefore, Uniqlo continued to recruit well-known designers from the industry, such as Alexander Wang, JW Anderson and Ines de la Fressange, for special temporary collections. Finally, the French creative director of the women's line at Hermès, Christophe Lemaire, designed the Uniqlo U line since 2016.

Uniqlo's strategy based on big names in the fashion industry has been expanded with the sponsorship of athletes such as the wheelchair tennis champions Shingo Kunieda and Gordon Reid in 2009 and 2017, respectively, the snowboarder Ayumu Hirano in 2018, the tennis player Kei Nishikori in 2011 and 2018, and golfer Adam Scott since 2014. As such, these athletes appear in Uniqlo's commercials and wear Uniqlo apparel

Figure 2. Novak Djokovic and Tadashi Yanai announcing their partnership (2012).

during their competitions. On the contrary, Uniqlo sells the outfit of their top athletes each season.

The position of Uniqlo toward its ambassadors is closely connected to Tadashi Yanai, and the official announcements are mostly made through him. In 2014, for instance, Tadashi Yanai posed with Adam Scott after he became World's number one golfer in front of calligraphy depicting the words "World's Number One". Uniqlo wishes to conserve this proximity to its athletes. At the end of Novak Djokovic's contract with Uniqlo, Tadashi Yanai wrote him a letter to thank him for the collaboration they shared (Figure 2).

Made for All

The difficulties in the integration of Uniqlo as a major retailer in the international market due to the lack of brand awareness were combined with a second issue: the sizing of clothing. While both the Japanese and the American markets can easily appreciate casual intemporal clothing, the average measurement of an American adult differs a lot from the Japanese adult. The clothes to be sold in Europe and in the US were then upsized sloppily, which is repulsive for a customer who does not want to try every T-shirt he buys to be sure they all fit.

A 2019 study by the competition analysis tool Retview highlighted the improvement in this matter, comparing an assortment mix of the three main clothing retailers H&M, Zara and Uniqlo. Where the choice of repartition of products between different clothing categories is somewhat similar in all three retailers, Uniqlo proposes on average every product in 3.5 sizes and 3.3 colors. This emphasis on the choice for the customer and the low prices set by Uniqlo make the customer experience at Uniqlo not only affordable but also accessible, since it is likely that a customer will find something appropriate based on his/her preferences and available products (Retview, 2019) (Figure 3).

To better find these various sizes and colors of products efficiently, UNIQLO stores are standardized to form a brand identity and to allow every customer to find what he/she needs wherever he/she may be in the world. While the initial regular stores are 800 square meters, UNIQLO opened stores of 1650 square meters or even 3300 square meters for its flagship outside Japan. Small stores of 150 square meters also exist to distribute the main products of the season.

Average number of sizes available Retviews. Womenswear, 2019

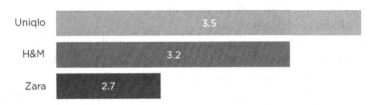

RETVIEWS

Average number of colors Retviews. Womenswear, 2019

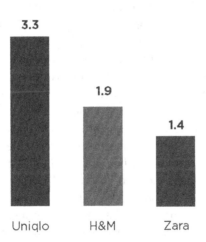

RETVIEWS

Figure 3. Review analysis comparing the products available at H&M, Zara and Uniqlo. Retviews (2020). https://retviews.com/blog/focus/uniqlo-competitors/ Accessed November 11, 2020.

Uniqlo and Mass Markets

The differentiation in colors and sizes alongside the collaborations with designers improved the brand awareness, especially internationally as Uniqlo stores opening in European capitals work well, particularly in Russia, France and the United Kingdom, as the consumer demand for Uniqlo products is steady.

However, the European market is proportionately a small generator of Uniqlo's profit, representing 90 billion yen for the year 2018 matched by the profit in North America, compared to the massive revenue of sales in Japan which exceeded 850 billion yen; also impressive is the popularity of Uniqlo in Greater China (440 billion yen), Southeast Asia & Oceania (140 million yen) and South Korea (140 billion yen).

While the profit of Uniqlo is the same in Europe as in America, the market size differs and Uniqlo struggles to take over the American market compared to their competitors H&M and Zara and compared to the global size of the American market for clothing. The brand awareness is still too limited compared to the size of the market to be considered successful. Uniqlo faces limitations to enter the American market due to the size of the US. Since big cities are spread widely around the country, and mall stores are a declining activity in the US, Uniqlo cannot be everywhere.

To overcome this difficulty, Uniqlo focuses on its flagship stores, located in prime touristic hubs such as New York City (on 5th Street and Broadway) or Los Angeles (downtown Santa Monica or Beverly Center). Americans can in this way observe Uniqlo's products in gigantic and beautiful stores, before ordering these products online once home. Uniqlo takes advantage of the habit of Americans to consume online. Indeed, in all major areas in which Uniqlo has settled, the online sales ratio is the highest in North America, close to 20% of all Uniqlo sales compared to Greater China (15%), Europe (10%), Japan (7%), South Korea and Southeast Asia and Oceania (5%) (Fast Retailing financial reports, 2018).

As of 2018, the international operations of Uniqlo are for the first time more profitable than the revenues of Uniqlo on Japanese territory. This overtaking is mostly due to the rise of Uniqlo in Greater China, functioning as the second main area of business. In 2011, 52 stores were opened in China and 673 at the end of 2018 (768 for the Greater China area). Uniqlo understood the importance of settling aggressively in the biggest markets in the world population-wise.

Uniqlo strategists compare today's India to China at the end of the 1990s, with an aging textile industry requiring new industrial practices to be effective (Economic Times India 2019). Uniqlo opened its first store in New Delhi, India, in Fall 2019 and places a lot of hope in this new market that is for now relatively unexplored by the competitors H&M and Zara (about 30 and 20 stores, respectively). In an interview in June 2019, Tadashi Yanai stated that "The budget is unlimited when it comes to investment (in India) and there is no capping." In a booming country with over 1.3 billion inhabitants, conquering the Indian market would increase the domination of Uniqlo over its competitors in the Asian market as the reference in the field of casual clothing at an accessible price.

Questions

1. What strategies can help Uniqlo succeed in the Indian market?
2. Why was the first entrance in the European and American markets mitigated in the early 2000s?
3. How is the figure of Tadashi Yanai significant in the retail industry?

References

Economic Times India (2019). Uniqlo ready with "unlimited investment" for its India play. https://economictimes.indiatimes.com/industry/cons-products/garments-/-textiles/uniqlo-ready-with-unlimited-investment-for-its-india-play/articleshow/69967006.cms.

Fast Retailing (2018). Annual reports. *https://www.fastretailing.com/eng/ir/library/pdf/ar2018_en.pdf.*

Fast Retailing (2019). Tadashi Yanai. *https://www.fastretailing.com/eng/about/company/profile_yanai.html.*

Haghirian, P. (2014). Case Studies in Asian Management, *World Scientific 2013*

Obstfeld, M. (2009). Time of Troubles: The Yen and Japan's Economy, 1985–2008. Published in In *Koichi Hamada, Anil Kashyap, and David Weinstein (eds.), Japan's Bubble, Deflation, and Long-Term Stagnation. Cambridge, MA: MIT Press, 2010.* http://www.esri.go.jp/en/workshop/081211/081211_conference08.pdf.

Retviews (2019). Uniqlo Strategy — The Differences with Competitors H&M and Zara. https://retviews.com/fr/blog/focus/uniqlo-competitors/.

www.uniqlo.com (2020). https://www.uniqlo.com/jp/ja/. (Accessed on March 10, 2019).

© 2021 World Scientific Publishing Company
https://doi.org/10.1142/9789811231032_0004

Case 4

Uber's Failure in Southeast Asia: How a Local Champion Won the Fight Against the Global Titan

Moritz Lahme

The Share Economy

The sharing economy became widely recognized all over the world. Young and innovative companies became serious rivals to well-established, traditional industries in the respective markets. The concept of sharing as a business model, which is also known as share economy or collaborative economy, is based on new technology that facilitates the exchanged access of goods or services between two or more parties (Miller, 2019). Through shared marketplaces, collaborative platforms, or peer-to-peer applications as communication platforms, and the increasing accessibility of the internet and mobile technology, these parties can share value from an underutilized service or asset. Private vehicles for example go unused 95% of their lifetime, making it beneficial for car owners to share their unused vehicles with others in need for a lower rate than traditional car rental services.

Another example that highlights the benefits of the sharing economy is the lodging sharing service Airbnb. As homeowners make use of spare bedrooms or even their whole house by listing and sharing it with guests through the Airbnb platform, rates are reportedly 30–60% cheaper than hotel rates around the world due to cost advantages over hotel space.

On the one hand, homeowners earn rental money, while on the other hand, it provides travelers easy access to renting private homes. Driven primarily by the further growth of Uber, Airbnb and other disruptive innovations, the sharing economy is expected to grow from US$14 billion in 2014 to a forecasted US$335 billion by 2025 (Chappelow, 2019).

The ride-sharing economy, which did not even exist a decade ago was said to be worth US$61.3 billion in 2018 and is expected to grow up to US$218 billion in 2025, at an annual growth rate of almost 20% (Dyson, 2018). This growth is mainly driven by the rise of on-demand transportation services, global urbanization, employment opportunities and a decreasing rate of car ownership among younger generations. Due to lucrative market opportunities, boundless growth potential and expected user base increase of ride-hailing services, many competitors entered the market across the globe. Key players operating in the global ride-sharing market besides Uber now include Lyft, Grab, Didi Chuxing, OLA Share and more.

Uber Disrupting the Transportation Industry

Uber's story began in Paris in 2008 when Travis Kalanick and Garrett Camp were attending an annual tech conference. Both previously sold start-ups they co-founded in return for large sums of money. One cold winter night during the conference in Paris, when Kalanick and Camp had trouble getting a cab, the initial idea of Uber was born. When Camp returned to San Francisco, he continued working on the idea and soon developed the first prototype for UberCab. In summer 2009, Camp persuaded his friend Kalanick to join as UberCab's Chief Incubator, and soon after, the newly developed innovation was tested in New York City with only three cars. However, the official launch took place in San Francisco in May.

Hailing a taxi has never been easier since Uber launched its business in San Francisco. Just by simply clicking on a button, a ride could be ordered. Through GPS signals, the locations of both drivers and passengers were identified and the app provided additional information on how long the ride will take and how much it will cost. Additionally, the fare was automatically charged to the card on the user account. Customers loved the simplicity of ordering a taxi and the app's popularity was rising tremendously. In October 2010, Uber collected its first major funding of

US$1.25 million and in December that year Kalanick became CEO of the company (Blystone, 2019).

Since Uber launched its ride-hailing service in San Francisco in 2009, which enabled passengers to hail a vehicle using an online platform, it revolutionized the transportation industry and gained incredible popularity across the globe. One key factor of Uber's and its business model's success lies in its simplicity: Users benefit from a fast, efficient, personal and user-friendly experience when using the app and hailing a vehicle. Without calling or queuing up for a taxi, ride-sharing platforms provide a more comfortable way of transportation with their door-to-door services. Introducing a rating system for both passenger and driver, Uber helped to better establish trust between the two unknown parties, also making this service safer than traditional taxis. With its user-friendly application and simple business model, Uber has set new and high standards for other businesses in the growing sharing economy.

Expanding Overseas

In February 2011, Uber announced it had raised another US$11 million in series A funding. With new money, the company started to expand throughout its home country, beginning with New York City, Seattle, Boston and Chicago. Later that year, Uber expanded beyond the United States, by launching its services in Paris. Three years later, Uber was launched internationally in the same city where the initial idea was born. Soon after, the company continued its global expansion and went into Canada, Mexico, Taiwan and the UK. With the help of regular funding rounds, Uber kept expanding and soon claimed to launch its application in a new city each day.

Due to its growing population and rising urbanization, the largest growth in ride-sharing is expected in the Asian market (Robert Curley, 2019). In 2017, 70% of the 16 billion global rides were completed in Asia, making the continent the world's largest ride-hailing market (Vulcan Post, 2018). Southeast Asia (SE-Asia) especially, home to about 640 million people, plays an important role due to its growing population and increasing urbanization. Additionally, emerging markets like Cambodia and Myanmar and megacities like Bangkok, Jakarta and Manila contribute to the significance of the SE-Asia region. Traffic in these cities is among the worst in the world and during rush hour, citizens suffer from notorious traffic jams. Furthermore, the growth of smartphone usage in the region is among the fastest throughout the globe and more than 400 million people are estimated to own one by 2020.

Grab's First Steps

Despite Uber being the first online platform offering taxi-hailing services, the American company was not the first one in the SE-Asia region. Using taxis was a serious problem in many Asian countries. Public transport is not always available or reliable, and taxi companies were not very well organized and often not considered a safe option to get from one place to another. It is therefore not a surprise that Uber's business model had created interest in many other markets.

Anthony Tan, along with co-founder Tan Hooi Ling, established MyTeksi in Kuala Lumpur in 2011. GrabTaxi, which was later rebranded as Grab, launched in Malaysia in 2012 as a third-party taxi e-hailing platform. Talking about the early stages of his company, Tan said, "We started GrabTaxi because the taxi system in Malaysia was a mess. Drivers weren't making enough money and hated their jobs. Women couldn't go around safely. We needed to do something about it" (Freischlad, 2015).

The company's mission was clear: Improving safety and accessibility of transportation as well as lives of passengers and drivers. This includes making travelling easier and safer for passengers, especially for women. Co-founder Tan Hooi Ling, who grew up in Malaysia, also recalled how she constantly tried to convince her parents to let her ride in a taxi when she was a teenager. Additionally, by building and providing a platform that successfully matched the highly underutilized supply to demand, Grab's business model aimed to solve the supply–demand disparity in major SE-Asian cities (Mei and Dula, 2016).

But, Grab's first steps in the new ride-sharing market were far from smooth. Anthony Tan went door to door trying to convince the biggest local taxi companies in Kuala Lumpur to try his product and persuade them about the effectiveness of his new business model. Drivers were not necessarily tech-affine and were rather unwilling to get into it. The fifth taxi company, which was a lot smaller, only operating a fleet of 30 taxis, gave him the chance to try out Grab's new mobile application, and in June 2012, the company finally launched SE-Asia's first taxi-hailing app.

"Grabbing" SE-Asia

Soon after the app went live, Grab expanded into Singapore in early 2013, partnering up with taxi companies to quickly expand its fleet. In the following year, the company expanded its business model offering Uber-like ride-sharing services for private vehicle owners and passengers, which the company called GrabCar. Besides Singapore, Grab entered the markets in the Philippines, Thailand, Vietnam and Indonesia in 2013 and 2014. In 2017, Grab introduced its services to the markets in Myanmar and Cambodia, which are both listed among the fastest growing economies in the region (Kazi, 2018). Within only six years, Grab managed to successfully enter eight markets in the SE-Asia region.

Aiming to benefit from the booming SE-Asian market and become the market leader, Uber entered the region with the launch of its application in Singapore in early 2013. As Grab was already starting to expand into other countries, Uber followed and entered the same markets. However, in each country, Grab was quicker and could beat Uber by a few months. Nevertheless, Uber managed to gain significant market shares and soon became the market leader in the region. Therefore, Uber focused on securing the dominant position in the major countries and kept investing to fight the war against local competitor Grab (Davis, 2018).

Focusing on fast international expansion across SE-Asia, Grab aggressively used consumer promotions and provider incentives, which drained much of Grab's initial US$90 million funding that the company could secure until October 2014. To continue its growth and support expansion, Grab frequently returned to the capital markets collecting more money from investors. In December 2014, Grab managed to raise US$250 million in series D funding, invested in full by the Japanese telecom company SoftBank. According to Grab, SoftBank's investment was the largest investment made in a SE-Asian internet company on public record. With new money from SoftBank, Grab was able to continue its aggressive strategy and became more and more prominent as market shares were increasing.

Fighting the global giant Uber, and expanding into new markets, was burning a lot of cash, which is why Grab raised another US$350 million in series E funding in August 2015 from a range of investors including Chinese ride-hailing company Didi Cuxing and China Investment Corporation. In September the following year, Grab again secured US$750 million from SoftBank, Didi and Honda (Wikipedia, 2019).

Compared to Grab, Uber invested US$700 million in the region according to an internal e-mail (Khosrowshahi, 2018). Clearly, Grab was burning a lot more cash fighting this bruising price war than its giant American competitor.

Nevertheless, besides advertisements, vouchers and promotions, Grab focused on serving demand by fulfilling local interests and developing localized versions of its ride-sharing app. The overall goal was to keep fighting, achieve rapid user growth throughout the region, overtake Uber and eventually become the market leader.

Think Global, Act Local

As Grab fought and grew aggressively over the years, it kept developing and experimenting with localized product enhancements and services. As motorbikes and scooters are the predominant form of transportation in SE-Asian cities, to weave in and out of monstrous traffic jams, the company launched GrabBike in November 2014 in Ho Chi Minh City, Jakarta, and other major cities. In the Philippines, Grab even included "trikes" in its transportation fleet, as many locals used them regularly. Uber launched its motorbike and scooter service, which the company called UberMOTO, as a pilot program in Bangkok in early 2016. Introducing a motorcycle service marked the first time that the US-based company had offered rides on two-wheeled vehicles (Toor, 2016).

Coming from the US, Uber was used to American customers who use credit cards or other cashless payment methods on a daily basis. For that reason, Uber only offered cashless payment options in Asia when entering the market. Grab on the other contrary accepted cash as well as credit card payments from the beginning. Two years after its launch, Uber introduced and offered cash payments to its customers as well. Talking about localization, head of Grab Singapore Mr. Lim Kell Jay said in an interview, "Every city is different, even within the same country, so you need to understand all those nuances to serve your customers better" (Ng, 2018). He truly believed that local understanding of the market is something that cannot be underestimated. Therefore, the company carved out a niche for itself and intensely focused on local needs and cultures.

As Uber became a global player, designed for the global market, smaller changes and adjustments in the app had greater effects and took more time, especially in the decision-making process. Because Uber is using one single app for all global users, changing any functionality involves complicated IT changes which happen at a headquarters level. Local competitor Grab on the other contrary had local people and engineering teams on the ground, more local know-how about specific customer needs and the advantage of being much faster in the decision-making process. In addition, it has designed its mobile app to fit individual markets in which languages and payment platforms are adapted accordingly.

Connecting with the Community

Grab also got involved in many local social initiatives and started its own social campaigns. During Ramadan in 2018, for instance, Grab introduced GrabBus in Indonesia. The feature was launched to provide free shuttle services for Muslims living in the outskirts of the city to Jakarta's largest mosque (Ng, 2018). The company also launched a program that aims to develop life skills and foster a spirit of entrepreneurship among the children of its drivers, called GrabSchool (Grab, 2015). In 2016, Grab introduced free personal accident insurance that covers all GrabCar and GrabBike passengers in case an accident occurs. To increase safety for both female drivers and passengers who are at greater risk of violence, Grab installed CCTV cameras in the cars of women drivers and introduced the Share-My-Ride feature. With the latter, passengers are able to share their rides with loved ones to let them know their whereabouts. Additionally, Grab included an emergency button in its app that connects passengers with the nearest police department in case of an emergency (Ng, 2018).

Collaboration with National Authorities

In general, Grab collaborated and worked closely together with local and municipal governments. In accordance with its mission, the company aims to improve transportation-related issues, most importantly the notorious traffic congestion. Therefore, the company announced in 2015 that it would partner up with The World Bank's Open Traffic project, providing real-time data streaming that reported service volume, location tracking and historical journey times. Examining historical data could help transportation departments to better understand congestion patterns, plan transportation infrastructure, and improve emergency response and disaster preparation (Lin and Dula, 2016).

Uber followed its American approach and did not actively seek out and work with local and municipal regulators, which worked well for the company in the US. In Europe and Asia, however, the company encountered unplanned difficulties as the regulatory framework was not as kind or welcoming as Uber had hoped. In the Philippines, national authorities punished Uber with a one-month suspension in 2017, after the company disregarded an order to not accept any more drivers on its platform. But, the ride-hailing giant fought back, filed a motion and continued operations until the motion was resolved. Unlike Uber, Grab complied with the orders and stopped recruiting and accepting new drivers (Tan, 2017).

Uber and Grab Fighting Bad Publicity

The more popular and well-known Uber became, the more scandals affected the company's global reputation. Particularly in 2017, the company was facing a lot of negative publicity in its home-base country. As president Trump enforced the refugee ban in 2017, taxi companies showed solidarity and joined protestors by refusing to pick up passengers arriving at JFK airport in New York City. Uber, however, did not join the protests and continued operating by picking up passengers arriving at the airport. As a consequence, Uber sparked a nationwide #DeleteUber campaign. Soon after, a video went viral, showing former CEO Kalanick arguing and yelling at an Uber driver after he confronted Kalanick about salary cuts. In addition, former Uber engineer Susan Fowler accused the firm of fostering a sexist and misogynistic corporate culture. Consequently, Uber was repeatedly in the news with increasing cases of sexual assault, having serious difficulties with sexual harassment and a potentially broken culture in the company. Through social media, news spread all over the internet and Uber's global image was severely damaged.

However, Uber has also been making headlines internationally. In 2014, Uber was banned for a limited time in India by the national transportation department, after an Uber driver allegedly raped a female passenger. Consequently, Uber has been accused of failing to conduct adequate checks on its drivers. Some executives at Uber even believed the woman was fraudulently claiming that she had been raped in collusion with one of the company's rivals and gained access to the woman's medical records. The victim then filed a lawsuit for intrusion into private affairs, public disclosure of private facts and defamation, which was settled in 2017 without revealing the terms (Moyer, 2017). Moreover, in Singapore, Uber bought more than 1,000 used cars that were previously recalled from Honda due to an electrical component that can overheat and catch fire. As owning a car in Singapore is very expensive, Uber had trouble recruiting enough drivers when entering the market in the city-state. To solve this problem, the company was leasing these cars to potential drivers. Although Uber executives knew about the technical issues, the company continued leasing these defective vehicles to drivers without warning them of the safety issue. In January 2017, one of these cars spouted flames from its dashboard after the driver just dropped off a passenger (Wamsley, 2017).

Grab was also facing issues between drivers and passengers with the company's first case appearing in September 2016, after a female passenger in Singapore was sexually assaulted by a Grab driver after she fell asleep during the ride. Several similar incidents occurred afterward in Thailand, Malaysia and Indonesia in the following years (Wikipedia, 2019).

Grab Becoming the Leader of the Market

In 2015, Grab eventually overtook Uber as the company became more and more prominent in its home markets and gained significant market shares. Meanwhile, Uber stopped heavily investing in the region and focused on securing as much market share as possible. Although Uber decreased investments in the SE-Asia region, the American company still followed Grab into markets in Cambodia and Myanmar in 2017. Regarding Uber's investments, the company managed to spend just enough money to stay competitive and hinder Grab from tipping the market to their platform. Especially in platform competition, tipping the market is often the case, due to network effects that lead to winner-takes-it-all dynamics. Uber's goal seemed to be to neither gain nor lose market shares in the respective countries and stay a major player in the region (Davis, 2018).

Uber Fighting Many Battles

Besides losing market shares to Grab in SE-Asia, Uber's management saw itself confronted with many battles throughout the world. Even in its home country, the pressure on Uber increased after Lyft launched its ride-hailing application and quickly grew within the US. Although Uber controls the majority of the US ride-hailing market, competitor Lyft has eaten into Uber's US market shares (Molla, 2018).

In Europe, licensed taxi drivers protested and complained that the American app presented them with unfair competition. Some of these protests brought large parts of bustling cities to a grinding halt. As a result, regulators in several countries banned Uber or some of its services, including Hungary and Bulgaria where the app has been banned completely. Some services have been banned in cities across France, Italy, Finland, Germany and the Netherlands. But, regulators were not the only ones who slowed Uber down in Europe; in Europe, as all around the world, several competitors entered the market over the years, including Yandex in Russia (Shead, 2019).

Uber Selling Businesses in China and Russia

In August 2016, Uber left the Chinese market selling its business to the local competitor Didi Chuxing after a brutal battle between the two apps. As part of the deal, the US-based firm took a 17.5% share in the combined company. The main reason for retreating from the Chinese market was Uber losing more than US$1 billion a year after the company had already spent US$2 billion in two years trying to battle Didi. In addition, Didi Chuxing claimed to have nearly 80% of market share (Kharpal, 2016), which made it too expensive for Uber to keep fighting. By retreating from the Chinese market, Uber lost the opportunity to provide and sell their services in the world's second largest economy, but gained a sizeable stake in the biggest ride-sharing player with a customer base of more than 750 million people. However, the value of Uber's stake in Didi was estimated at US$5.97 billion as of the end of 2017 and US$7.95 billion at the end of 2018, which is nearly a jump on paper of US$2 billion in only one year (Russell, 2019).

In July 2017, Uber also retreated from the Russian market, forming a joint venture with local rival Yandex. Like in China, the local competitor Yandex was the dominant one in the Russian market. The new firm will be majority owned by local rival Yandex, whereas Uber took 36.6% in shares worth around US$1.4 billion. Unlike the Didi deal, however, Uber will remain an active participant in its new Russian investment, and its users in the country will continue to use the same app as the rest of the world (Hern, 2017). Russia's population of more than 140 million makes an increase of business highly likely which will increase Uber's value within it (Russell, 2019).

Uber Selling Its SE-Asian Business to Grab

Early in 2018, SoftBank's Vision Fund invested US$10 billion in Uber, which increased suspicion of a shake-up in Asia's ride-hailing industry. As SoftBank also owns stakes in Grab, executives were pushing for this deal and favoring consolidation after the money-burning price war between the two competitors (Zaveri and Bosa, 2019). As both sides were relying heavily on discounts and promotions fighting this bruising price war, profit margins were driven down drastically.

Eventually, in March 2018, Uber sold its SE-Asian business valued at US$6 billion to its bigger regional rival Grab. In return, Uber will take 27.5% stake in the Singapore-based company and Uber CEO Dara Khosrowshahi will join Grab's board. That stake, worth more than US$1.6 billion, is a strong return considering that Uber claimed to have invested $700 million in SE-Asia over the years (Russell, 2019). In 2019, Grab was valued at US$14 billion, making Uber's stakes already worth more than US$3.22 billion (Russell, 2019). Consolidating businesses will help Grab to further develop and expand its meal delivery service which will merge with UberEats. Additionally, acquiring Uber's businesses in the region will strengthen Grab's position against new competitors in the market like Go-Jek in Indonesia.

Particularly for companies considering a potential IPO to turn out to be successful, the business needs to be profitable in the long run and high profit margins are necessary. Therefore, suspicions arose that Uber was planning an IPO and leaving unprofitable markets where the company was burning too much cash. However, in response to these suspicions after leaving the SE-Asian market, CEO Dara Khosrowshahi (2018) wrote the following in an internal e-mail:

"It is fair to ask whether consolidation is now the strategy of the day, given this is the third deal of its kind, from China to Russia and now Southeast Asia. The answer is no. One of the potential dangers of our global strategy is that we take on too many battles across too many fronts and with too many competitors. This transaction now puts us in a position to compete with real focus and weight in the core markets where we operate, while giving us valuable and growing equity stakes in a number of big and important markets where we don't. While M&A will always be an important value-creation tool for our company, going forward we will be focused on organic growth — growth that comes from building the best products, services and technology in the world, and re-building our brand into the mobility brand that riders, cities and drivers want to support and partner with" (Khosrowshahi, 2018).

Although, leaving the SE-Asian market will help Uber become more profitable, it is also yet another retreat from an important and promising international market for the US-based company.

Outlook — How Grab is Becoming a "Super-App"

Within a span of seven years, Grab has introduced more than 10 on-demand ride-hailing services across eight countries in the SE-Asia region, basically becoming a mobile-based app to hire anything that rides on wheels. These hailing services include taxis, private cars, carpooling, bicycle sharing, shuttle services and bike taxis. In 2019, the application processed over six million ride orders with more than 2.8 million drivers every day. But, Grab's vision goes way beyond being just a ride-sharing platform. The company is following the everyday super app model with role models like Alipay or WeChat. Hence, it has forayed into multiple consumer service sectors such as hotel booking services, on-demand video platform, ticket purchasing, food ordering and grocery shopping, besides offering financial services.

In January 2016, Grab launched its QR-based mobile payments service GrabPay. Besides paying for Grab rides, users can pay for in-store purchases, food deliveries and fund transfers. The company went even further and currently provides loans to small and medium-sized companies and micro-insurances for drivers in Singapore as well. According to Grab, it has also built a merchant network comprising more than 6,000 merchants and GrabPay even allows customers to pay online on well-known e-commerce platforms such as Qoo10 and 11Street. To increase customer satisfaction, GrabPay started offering a pay later option, which allows users to pay for all Grab services at the end of the month without any additional fee.

Business Growth and Market Expansion

In May 2018, Grab officially launched its food delivery business as part of its strategy to become an everyday everything super app. With GrabFood, the company hopes to gain a great share in the SE-Asian food delivery market, which it expects to grow over six times into a US$13 billion market by 2022. The food delivery service is available in six countries and over 200 cities in the region.

In collaboration with Indonesia-headquartered grocery delivery provider HappyFresh, Grab launched its own grocery delivery service GrabFresh in July 2018. The idea is that Grab drivers can choose to deliver food or groceries between driving passengers to their destination. Currently, the service is only available in the greater Jakarta region, but plans to roll it out to other cities including Bangkok and Kuala Lumpur and plans to enter more Asian cities do already exist.

In the beginning of 2019, Grab added four new industries: Hotel booking, on-demand video streaming, ticket purchasing and trip planning. So far, it is only available for customers in Singapore, but Grab is planning to roll out these services to all users in its open super app throughout the year as well. Therefore, the company partnered up with hospitality platforms like Booking.com or video on-demand streaming platforms HOOQ and BookMyShow (Entrepreneur Asia Pacific, 2019). Just recently, at the end of 2019, Grab also announced an alliance with Singapore Telecommunications (Singtel) to apply for a digital full banking license. With this collaboration, both companies aim to offer a variety of digital banking services. Singtel is the largest telecom operator in the region and next to Grab among the most popular and well-known brands in SE-Asia. What both companies combine is the expansion outside their traditional businesses (Channel News Asia, 2019). By collaborating with Singtel to increase financial services, Grab will enlarge its chances to impact the SE-Asian region even more in the future.

Questions

1. Which strategies did Uber and Grab follow to expand their business throughout SE-Asia?
2. What similarities and differences can be identified in the strategies of the two companies?

3. Why did Uber lose its leading position in the SE-Asian region?
4. Including all involved companies and stakeholders, who in your opinion won in the end?

References

Blystone, D. (2019). The Story of Uber. https://www.investopedia.com/articles/personal-finance/111015/story-uber.asp. (Accessed on December 12, 2020).

Channel News Asia (2019). Singtel to team up with Grab for Singapore digital bank licence. https://www.channelnewsasia.com/news/business/grab-singtel-singapore-digital-banking-licence-partnership-12219220. (Accessed on December 12, 2020).

Chappelow, J. (2019). Sharing Economy. https://www.investopedia.com/terms/s/sharing-economy.asp. (Accessed on December 12, 2020).

Davis, J. (2018). The Real Story Behind Uber's Exit from Southeast Asia. https://knowledge.insead.edu/entrepreneurship/the-real-story-behind-ubers-exit-from-southeast-asia-10096. (Accessed on December 12, 2020).

Dyson, M. (2018). Ride-sharing market to hit $218bn by 2025. https://www.businesstravelnewseurope.com/Ground-Transport/Ride-sharing-market-to-hit-218bn-by-2025. (Accessed on December 12, 2020).

Entrepreneur Asia Pacific (2019). How Grab is Becoming an Everyday, Everything App in Southeast Asia. https://www.entrepreneur.com/article/334690. (Accessed on December 12, 2020).

Freischlad, N. (2015). Three years, $340M funding, millions of users: GrabTaxi's Anthony Tan reflects on the journey. https://www.techinasia.com/3-years-4-funding-rounds-grabtaxis-anthony-tan-reflects-journey. (Accessed on December 12, 2020).

Grab, (2015). GrabTaxi launches GrabSchool to teach drivers' children entrepreneurship and life skills. https://tinyurl.com/ycuoc8x2. (Accessed on December 12, 2020).

Hern, A. (2017). Uber stages retreat in Russia as it merges with rival Yandex. https://www.theguardian.com/technology/2017/jul/13/uber-russia-yandex-chinese-business. (Accessed on December 12, 2020).

Kazi, M. (2018). Cambodia among fastest growing economies in region: McKinsey. https://www.khmertimeskh.com/535015/cambodia-among-fastest-growing-economies-in-region-mckinsey/. (Accessed on December 12, 2020).

Kharpal, A. (2016). 5 reasons why Uber sold its China business to Didi Chuxing. https://www.cnbc.com/2016/08/01/5-reasons-why-uber-sold-its-china-business-to-didi-chuxing.html. (Accessed on December 12, 2020).

Khosrowshahi, D. (2018). A New Future for Uber and Grab in Southeast Asia. https://www.uber.com/newsroom/uber-grab/. (Accessed on December 12, 2020).

Mei, L. and Dula, C. (2016). Grab Taxi: Navigating New Frontiers — A drive for growth in the sharing economy. https://cmp.smu.edu.sg/sites/cmp.smu.edu.sg/files/pdf/8.Grab%20Taxi.pdf. (Accessed on December 12, 2020).

Miller, D. (2019). The Sharing Economy and How it Is Changing Industries. https://www.thebalancesmb.com/the-sharing-economy-and-how-it-changes-industries-4172234. (Accessed on December 12, 2020).

Molla, R. (2018). Lyft has eaten into Uber's U.S. market share, new data suggests. https://www.vox.com/2018/12/12/18134882/lyft-uber-ride-car-market-share. (Accessed on December 12, 2020).

Moyer, E. (2017). Uber settles lawsuit over rape victim's medical records. https://www.cnet.com/news/uber-medical-records-rape-lawsuit-india/. (Accessed on December 12, 2020).

Ng, D. (2018). How Uber, valued at billions, was sent packing by a start-up in Singapore Read more at https://www.channelnewsasia.com/news/cnainsider/uber-grab-singapore-ride-hailing-southeast-asia-private-hire-10630396. (Accessed on December 12, 2020).

Robert, C. (2019). Global ride sharing industry valued at more than $61 Billion. https://www.businesstraveller.com/business-travel/2019/01/04/value-of-global-ride-sharing-industry-estimated-at-more-than-61-billion/. (Accessed on December 12, 2020).

Russell, J. (2019). Uber has already made billions from its exits in China, Russia and Southeast Asia. https://tinyurl.com/yafd6jur. (Accessed on December 12, 2020).

Shead, S. (2019). Uber's Rocky Road To Growth In Europe: Regulators, Rivals and Riots. https://www.forbes.com/sites/samshead/2019/05/10/ubers-rocky-road-to-growth-in-europe-regulators-rivals-and-riots/. (Accessed on December 12, 2020).

Tan, Y. (2017). The fight between Uber and the Philippines is on. https://mashable.com/2017/08/15/uber-philippines-resuming/. (Accessed on December 12, 2020).

Toor, A. (2016). Uber launches its first motorcycle service. https://www.theverge.com/2016/2/24/11104394/uber-motorcycle-service-bangkok-ubermoto. (Accessed on December 12, 2020).

Vulcan Post. (2018). Asia Is The World's Largest Ride-Hailing Market With Over 70% Share — Grab Dominates SEA. https://vulcanpost.com/647224/asia-worlds-largest-ride-hailing-market/. (Accessed on December 12, 2020).

Wamsley, L. (2017). Uber Knowingly Leased Unsafe Cars To Its Drivers In Singapore, Report Says. https://www.npr.org/sections/thetwo-way/2017/08/04/541692151/uber-knowingly-leased-unsafe-cars-to-its-drivers-in-singapore-report-says. (Accessed on December 12, 2020).

Wikipedia, (2019). Grab (Company) https://en.wikipedia.org/wiki/Grab_ (company)#Funding. (Accessed on December 12, 2020).

Zaveri, P. and Bosa, D. (2019). This map shows how SoftBank dominates the global ride-sharing industry. https://www.cnbc.com/2019/05/09/softbank-dominates-the-global-ride-sharing-industry.html (Accessed on December 12, 2020).

© 2021 World Scientific Publishing Company
https://doi.org/10.1142/9789811231032_0005

Case 5

PayPay's Entry into the Digital Payment Market of Japan

Tiantuo Yang

Introduction

Unlike other strong economies such as China and the USA, cashless payment movements are not progressing very smoothly in Japan. According to the Japan Times journalist Anne Beade's article, "Four out of five purchases are still made with cash in Japan, despite its reputation as a futuristic and innovative nation. In South Korea, some 90% of transactions are now digital, while Sweden aims to be a cashless society as early as 2023 (Beade, 2019)." Japanese people are reluctant to switch to cashless payment methods such as credit cards or third-party electronic payment services, because of their obsession with cash. There are multiple reasons behind Japanese people's fondness of cash, such as its simplicity, accountability and the fact that Japan is one of the safest countries in the world with less need to worry about cash being stolen. There is still plenty of potential space for development in the cashless payment services market, however, even with the existence of some strong players in the market such as Line Pay, Rakuten Pay and WeChat Pay. CoinDesk Japan editor Kubota referred to 2020 as the "Sengoku Period (Warring States Era)" for electronic payment applications in Japan (Kubota, 2020), as many huge companies stepped into the market, drastically intensifying the competition, yet no one is dominating.

The company this case study focuses on is PayPay, new blood in the cashless payment market, recently founded in 2018 by Softbank and Yahoo Japan. With no fears toward the existing competition, through extremely aggressive campaigns and advertisement, PayPay progressed rapidly and eventually became an unneglectable player in the market within a very short time.

The Digital Payment Market in Japan

One key characteristic of E-payment services is the ease of access, that it is very simple to become a user of these services; the customers only need to download the application on their smartphones and then they can pay with the QR code appearing on their smartphones at the stores which approve this payment service company.

Therefore, this ease of access leaves customers no difficulties or costs switching between service providers, keeping the companies' emphasis on how to keep their own customers from switching to their competitors. The competition between players in the E-payment market intensifies by nature due to this crucial characteristic of this business.

As mentioned above, despite Japanese people's reluctance toward cashless payments, there are indeed many choices available for E-payment services in Japan. LINE Pay, Rakuten Pay, WeChat Pay and AliPay were the most common digital payments companies before the entrance of PayPay (Figure 1). Each of these applications has a unique target customer base. For example, WeChat Pay is the product of one of the biggest companies in China, Tencent, with such a massive user base in China that makes China the market leader in the world of E-payment business. To take advantage of the existing user base and Chinese people's enthusiastic purchasing power when traveling abroad, WeChat Pay mainly targets Chinese tourists in Japan. By targeting Chinese tourists, WeChat Pay would seek collaboration with restaurants and stores that Chinese tourists

Figure 1.   The logo of PayPay (PayPay, 2020).

often visit, such as big shopping malls that allow tax refunds, classy Japanese-style restaurants and major convenience store branches.

Industrial Analysis of the Digital Market in Japan

According to Statista's market report on the digital market of Japan, "total transaction value in the Digital Payments segment amounts to US$173,136 m in 2020. Total transaction value is expected to show an annual growth rate (CAGR 2020–2023) of 4.1%, resulting in the total amount of US$195,440 m by 2023 (Statista Market Forecast, 2020)." From the statistics, the Japanese digital market appears to be a promising market with the digital transaction value consecutively increasing during the past years. As many strong players are competing in the market, the market is expected to grow continuously in the future. Meanwhile, the 4.1% annual growth rate of the market turns out to be a much more desirable one when considering the low inflation rate and the stagnating economy in Japan. It is plausible to assume that the electronic payment service business might develop into one of the few booming industries of Japan in the future (Figure 2).

Internationally, Japan was greatly surpassed by the United States and China in the digital payment market. According to Statista's market report on the global digital market, "with a total transaction value of

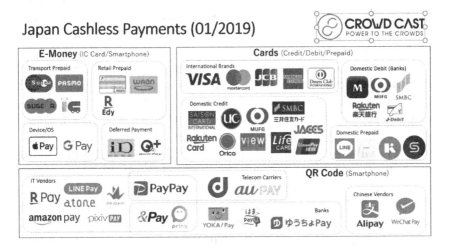

Figure 2. The translated version of Japan cashless payments map (Crowd Cast, 2019).

US$1,928,753 m in 2020, the highest value worldwide is reached in China (Statista Market Forecast, 2020)." The market report also states that the United States has the second highest value worldwide, with a total transaction value of US$1,058,288 m and Japan, with its transaction value of US$173,136 m, was ranked fourth in the world, slightly behind the UK's transaction value of US$176,077 m (Statista Market Forecast, 2020). The total digital transaction value of Japan was less than 10% of China's, leaving a lot of room for Japan to catch up on. As mentioned above, 80% of the purchases are still made by cash in Japan. Although the digital market in Japan generated promising figures, it is still outperformed by other strong economies and there is still potential for growth.

PayPay, A Joint Venture of Yahoo Japan and SoftBank

Despite it being a strong competitor now in the E-payment market, people tend to forget that PayPay is also the newest one. As the joint venture of Yahoo Japan, SoftBank and Paytm (an Indian company which is a minor investor and mainly provides technology of application designing for PayPay), PayPay Corporation was founded in June 2018. PayPay was founded at the time when WeChat Pay and Ali Pay had already taken over the E-payment service market in China and were expanding to Japan. Yahoo Japan's rivals, LINE and Rakuten, had already established their E-payment services, LINE Pay and Rakuten Pay. In order to compete with these competitors, Yahoo Japan and SoftBank established PayPay Corporation.

On SoftBank's official website, the company announced another reason behind the establishment of PayPay: "In Japan, cash (bank notes and coins) is still the mainstream payment methodology, with the current cashless payment ratio remaining at 20%. Consequently, the Japanese government is taking measures to raise the cashless payment ratio to 40% by 2025, with a long-term goal of 80%, the highest level globally. To aid these efforts, SoftBank and Yahoo Japan established PayPay Corporation in June 2018 and will launch its user-oriented payments platform in the Fall of 2018. This will promote the broader use of cashless payment in Japan and provide highly convenient services to both consumers and affiliated stores (Softbank, 2018)." SoftBank's announcement indicates that the company thinks the cashless payment market is underperforming with only a 20% payment ratio, and as the government is aiming to raise the cashless payment ratio in both the short term and the long term through tax incentives, SoftBank saw an opportunity in the market and therefore established PayPay Corporation.

PayPay's Strengths in a Well-Established Market

PayPay's main business is third-party electronic payment services, which to some extent is nothing different from its competitors. PayPay first negotiates with stores to make them affiliated so that the customers can use PayPay as their payment method. The customers just need to download an application on their smartphones, link their bank accounts or credit cards with PayPay accounts, then they can pay with the QR code appearing on the application without the need of taking out any cash or cards. There is no service fee incurred for paying through PayPay. This smartphone QR code payment business model is nothing different from other E-payment service providers; however, for a company to succeed, it is important to have an advantage over its peers to stand out from the market.

Since the core business is not really different, it is important for PayPay to find its own strengths in other categories, just like how WeChat Pay and Ali Pay only target Chinese tourists and they provide unique premiums and convenience only for Chinese visitors. According to SoftBank's official announcement, "PayPay Corporation, SoftBank, Yahoo Japan and Paytm will expand the number of users by including the customer base of SoftBank, and "Yahoo! Wallet" which comprises approximately 40 million accounts. They will also deploy the platform using SoftBank's sales know-how, and develop a tailored service offering leveraging Paytm's technology. Their aim is for PayPay to become the top provider of smartphone payment services in terms of the number of users as well as affiliated stores (SoftBank, 2018)." The Announcement indicates that, instead of targeting certain groups of people like WeChat Pay or Ali Pay's business in Japan, PayPay aims to be the biggest E-payment provider in Japan with the most users and affiliated stores. This means PayPay is targeting a much larger and broader customer base in Japan. As a newcomer in the market without popularity, how could PayPay become the biggest player?

In SoftBank's official announcement launching PayPay, it did state some of PayPay's strengths (SoftBank, 2018):

1. *Expanding the user base by including the strong customer base of SoftBank and Yahoo! Wallet.*
2. *Initial set up costs are low as the merchant only needs to display the code inside the shop. In addition, the service will be free to affiliate stores for the first three years from its launch.*
3. *Customers can select from two types of payment methods, namely credit cards and electronic money.*
4. *Leverages Paytm's consumer-centric technology to build mobile payment system and expand mobile payment in Japan.*

In summary, SoftBank aims to expand from their old customer base, provide three-year free services for stores, choices of E-payments for customers and advanced technology for building a mobile payment system from their Indian investor, Paytm. However, none of these strengths SoftBank identified really made PayPay stand out, because these strengths did not really create a material difference in E-payment services. What really helped PayPay gain popularity and fame after its launch in October 2018 was the initial campaign that had nothing to do with any of the advantages SoftBank identified, but with something only SoftBank could easily provide, money.

PayPay's Rebating Campaign, Dumping Money into the Sea?

PayPay Corporation was established in June 2018, and they released their PayPay application to start E-payment services in October 2018. On December 4th, two months after they started the services, PayPay launched their first refunding campaign. This event was PayPay's first big advertising event after its entrance to the market, and the campaign was called "10 billion-yen rebating campaign" which was designed to be a three-month campaign, between December 2018 and March 2019.

The main idea behind this campaign was quite simple, just like the name. PayPay gave its customers money back for paying through the application, and they were going to give out 10 billion yen (about 92 million US dollars) in total. During the campaign, for every customer who purchased at a PayPay-affiliated store, using PayPay as their payment method, would automatically be given 20% of the transaction amount from PayPay. There was also a small chance (the percentage is higher for SoftBank and Yahoo Japan account holders) that PayPay would match the entirety of the transaction under 100 thousand yen, and the customer would get the entire amount of the transaction back. All the money given by PayPay would be through PayPay E-money, which could be used as normal money through PayPay. The company would continue giving its customers money back until they gave out all of the 10 billion yen. By conducting a simple and obvious rebating campaign, directly giving its users cash back upon every purchase they made through the application, PayPay aimed to acquire a large initial user base as well as use the campaign as a method of advertising that could last for three months.

PayPay never officially announced in public the reasons for directly investing such a huge amount of money into its rebating campaign of which the outcomes were not guaranteed. For example, there were few rules or mechanics to retain the users they gained through the event and make sure they stayed active on a weekly or daily basis. Even though all the money given to the users would be through credit on their PayPay application, PayPay imposed no additional limits beyond that and they did not require the users to stay active or do anything in repay after the e-money was spent. What PayPay and its investors did was a very courageous approach in that they were only focusing on gaining the user base initially, and aiming to gain profits in the long run.

Aggressive Market Entry: A Three-Month Campaign Turned into a Ten-Day Campaign

This 10-billion-yen campaign aimed to give PayPay a head start into the E-payment business by gathering an initial customer base for PayPay with a massive investment amount. The campaign, in some ways, was very successful, a bit too successful in fact.

When PayPay was first launched in Japan, there were only a few affiliated stores, especially considering the chain stores. Bic Camera, Family Mart and Kojima Pets were the only chain brands that accepted payment with PayPay. Among these three brands, Bic Camera was the only comprehensive department store where large-amount transactions could happen. The limited number of affiliated stores could be one of the reasons that PayPay thought they could support such an aggressive rebating campaign for three months.

Customers' passion was greatly underestimated by PayPay. The campaign became huge news and a popular event among the Japanese customers. During the campaign, Japanese people had no hesitance in using cashless payment services. The campaign even became the reason for a lot of people to do shopping in the affiliated stores of PayPay, considering how high the rebating percentage was. This campaign became a booster in business for PayPay's partners. For example, Bic Camera's business was so greatly boosted that the store was crowded every day throughout the event. Since Bic Camera is a comprehensive department store with various items on sale, customers went there for high-priced products such as laptops and cameras to fully take advantage of PayPay's campaign.

Not surprisingly, in less than ten days, the initial designated amount, 10 billion Japanese yen, ran out. PayPay had to call an end to the campaign, which was designed and planned to last for three months. For PayPay, a three-month campaign had turned into a ten-day campaign. It did gain a fair amount of popularity and recognition from the customers due to its generosity throughout these ten days that it became big news and advertising for this newly born corporation. However, it is also impossible not to question whether the effect of this campaign is greatly damaged or affected due to underestimating customers' activity and not setting a securing procedure in case the money ran out way too quickly. Although its generosity did gain some popularity for PayPay, the advertising effect was still greatly impacted considering a three-month and long-term advertisement became a 10-day short-term one.

After the Initial Campaign and the Second Round

Within the first four months after its launch, through literally dumping money directly into the market, PayPay gained 4 million users. According to business editor Yamakawa from CNET Japan, "it (PayPay) was considered as the fastest-growing business of any Yahoo Japan's companies in history (山川, 2019)." However, there was no evaluation of whether these four million users would continue being active with PayPay after they used all the E-money they got from the campaign. It is hard to tell, to what extent, the 10-billion-yen investment has helped PayPay in one of the world's most difficult markets of cashless payment services. In any case, the 10-billion-yen investment will be a long-term investment for PayPay, since it will take years to repay it. If the investors' current expectations for

PayPay are merely gaining popularity and users as fast as possible, even though the campaign only ended after ten days, the campaign did an effective job giving PayPay a head start into the E-payment services provider business.

The company has never officially announced in public whether they feel satisfied with the outcome of their initial campaign. At the same time, PayPay never ceased progressing in advertising and expanding the business. Only three months after the initial campaign, surprisingly, in February 2019, PayPay launched another 10-billion-yen rebating campaign. The second 10-billion-yen campaign was nothing too different from the first one except for a securing procedure which set the limit to the money given from PayPay to a 1000-yen maximum for one single transaction and a 50,000-yen maximum for a user per month. With the addition of this rule, the second campaign successfully lasted for three months and was completed in May 2019. For this campaign, apparently, the company was looking for a more sustainable way to give money to its customers rather than running out of money quickly like the first campaign. It is also important to note that the second campaign was launched by PayPay within three months after the beginning of the first campaign, which was before the planned ending date for the first campaign. The quickness of the second campaign and the implementation of the securing procedure, to some extent, reflect that the company was not satisfied with the outcome of its first campaign.

A Deeper Look into the Business: Comparison of PayPay with WeChat Pay and Ali Pay

As mentioned in the industrial analysis section, China has the world's highest digital payment transaction value, which is more than ten times that of Japan's. Behind China's prosperity in the cashless payment market, there are two companies leading the tide, Tencent and Alibaba, with their phenomenal products, WeChat Pay and Ali Pay, respectively.

One purpose behind Softbank and Yahoo Japan's creation of PayPay was to duplicate WeChat Pay's and Ali Pay's success in Japan. They aimed to create the WeChat Pay or Ali Pay of Japan. However, there is an important difference that makes it much more difficult for PayPay to replicate that success, no matter how much money Yahoo Japan and Softbank dump into the market. The difference is that WeChat Pay and Ali Pay were never born as digital payment companies, but merely byproducts of their successful businesses.

WeChat Pay was not introduced to the customers until several years after WeChat became the social network with most users in China. WeChat Pay was introduced as an additional feature of WeChat so that users of WeChat Pay became users of WeChat in the first place. Because of the massive user base, it is very easy for WeChat to incentivize its customers to use the feature within the same application, WeChat Pay. There was not a single time WeChat Pay was the core business of WeChat. WeChat is always the social network application it was invented to be, a place where its users text, socialize and communicate with each other. However, it is much easier for a social network company to maintain its users than a digital payment company. Users can download new payment software and pay with it within seconds, but they cannot easily switch to a new social network because of their friends, connections and messages in the old one. WeChat Pay would never have to launch a giveaway campaign like PayPay did to attract new users and maintain the old ones. It is a similar story for Ali Pay, as it is the designated payment method for Alibaba, the biggest e-commerce platform in China. People became users of Ali Pay to use Alibaba. Because they were never born as digital payment companies, WeChat Pay and Ali Pay easily gained users from their mother companies and have no worries about losing customers easily to other competitors. Bundling with features of their mother companies, WeChat Pay and Ali Pay generate unique and unexchangeable value compared to mere digital payment companies.

Although Yahoo Japan and SoftBank claimed to include and bring their users to PayPay, it was not a number comparable to that of WeChat or Alibaba. PayPay still needs to launch those aggressive campaigns and have advertisement consecutively to stay competitive and relevant in the market. There are no guarantees that PayPay's current users would stay "loyal" if there is a new competitor with better incentives and better advertisement.

Conclusion

In general, within the digital payment market, PayPay was progressing incredibly quickly. Considering the amount of investment PayPay acquired from Softbank and Yahoo Japan, as well as how aggressive it is in advertising and business expansion, PayPay is one of the pioneers and strongest competitors now in the market. Up to November 17, 2019,

PayPay had gained 20 million registered users with 1.7 million affiliated stores and a total of 300 million transactions were conducted through it. For a company that had only entered the market about a year earlier, these are very impressive and promising figures. However, these numbers are still tiny but improvable in light of the giant economy of Japan. It will be a very exciting thing to see if, in the future, PayPay could really make a difference to the cashless payment market in Japan and change Japanese people's ongoing fondness of cash, as WeChat Pay and Ali Pay have achieved in China.

Questions

1. What are the reasons behind Softbank and Yahoo Japan's foundation of PayPay, considering the fierce competition in the market and how cashless payment is progressing with difficulties in Japan?
2. Do you agree with PayPay's aggressive campaign approach that only focused on getting users within a short time?
3. Was PayPay's initial campaign successful or not? If yes, how would you explain its second campaign launched within three months after the initial one?
4. What is the future of PayPay? The renovator of Japan's cashless payment market, a strong but not dominant competitor in the market or completely out of business due to its inability to repay the huge initial investment?

References

Beade, A. (2019). *In High-Tech Japan, Cash Remains King, Defying Mobile Payments | The Japan Times.* [online] The Japan Times. https://www.businesstelegraph.co.uk/in-high-tech-japan-cash-remains-king-defying-mobile-payments-the-japan-times/. (Accessed on January 28, 2020).

Crowd Cast (2019). *Japan Cashless Payments Map.* [image] https://medium.com/tokyo-fintech/japan-cashless-payments-map-859f529b24ec. (Accessed on Jan uary 28, 2020).

PayPay (2020). *The Trademark of PayPay.* [image] https://paypay.ne.jp/. (Accessed on January 28, 2020).

SoftBank (2018). *SoftBank and Yahoo Japan JV to Launch "PayPay," Barcode-Based Smartphone Payment Services in Collaboration with India's Paytm in the Fall | Press Releases | News | About Us | SoftBank.* [online] SoftBank.

https://www.softbank.jp/en/corp/news/press/sbkk/2018/20180727_01/. (Accessed on January 28, 2020).

Statista Market Forecast (2020). *Digital Payments — Japan.* [online] Statista. https://www.statista.com/outlook/296/121/digital-payments/japan. (Accessed on January 28, 2020).

Kubota, D. (2020). Nantoka Pay wa tôta no jidai e — — 2020-nen no kyasshuresu kessai wo mitôsu dikaretto Shiraishi Yôsuke CTO | CoinDesk Japan [online] CoinDesk Japan. https://www.coindeskjapan.com/32975/ [Accessed 28 Jan. 2020].

Yamakawa, A. (2019). PayPay wa yafû shijô saisoku de seichô -- ofurain tor-ikomi meeku ryôiki de uriage 5000 oku en e. [online] CNET Japan. https://japan.cnet.com/article/35132255/ [Accessed 28 Jan. 2020].

Dealing with Crisis

© 2021 World Scientific Publishing Company
https://doi.org/10.1142/9789811231032_0006

Case 6

Kao Corporation and the Kanebo Skin Care Scandal

Valerie Olenberger

Introduction

"Kirei — Making Life Beautiful" is Kao Corporation's mission and it wants to enrich its customers' lives with its wide variation of products in the areas of consumer products business and chemical business. The consumer products business is divided into the beauty care business, consisting of prestige cosmetics, premium skin care products and hair care products; the human health care business, including products like functional health beverages, sanitary products and personal health products; and the fabric and home care business, with products like laundry detergents and household cleaners. The chemical business develops chemical products to fulfill the needs of the industry. The company owns a big portfolio of brands in each product area, the beauty care business being the biggest and bringing in the most sales. Worldwide, this includes brands like Sofina, Curél, Molton Brown, Sensai and one of its biggest, Kanebo (Kao Corporation, 2020) (see Figure 1).

Japanese corporations have huge structures where many companies and brands belong under the mother brand but are operating mostly on their own. In its cosmetics business, Kao owns over 50 brands alone, which usually work independently from each other. This gives Kao enormous power and the chance to be one of the top players on the cosmetics market but also comes with risks. On the international market, Kao as a

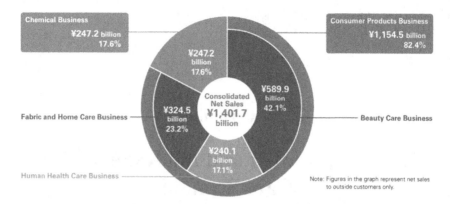

Figure 1.   Breakdown of business segment sales in 2014. (Kao Corporation, 2020).

Source: Kao Corporation (2014). Annual Report 2014. https://www.kao.com/global/en/investor-relations/library/reports/reports-backnumber/, Accessed November 11, 2020.

company is not well known and could not establish itself as a brand even though its products are already present worldwide. How can Kao Corporation use its strength to stay competitive on the global cosmetics market?

The Rise of Kao Group

The Kao company has a long history dating back to 1887. It was founded by Tomiro Nagase, who developed the first product of the company, the Kao Sekken, a high-quality toiletry soap. In the beginning, the company manufactured the soap under the name of Nihon Yuki Company. In 1902, the company completed the construction of its factory, which included all production processes from processing raw materials to packaging. Twenty years later, the production factory in Tokyo was established and is still used as an office space today. In the 1930s, the company opened its own laboratory to develop more household items. It introduced further hygiene products like shampoo, which changed the hair-washing routine in Japan and established the word "shampoo" in everyday life. From the sixties onward, the company started its expansion plan. Its first target country was Thailand, where it established the company Kao Industrial (Thailand) Co. Ltd. Soon after, the Taiwan-Kao Company was introduced, followed by Malaysia, Singapore and many other Southeast Asian countries. To also be more present on the European market, Kao established its first subsidiary in Spain in 1970 (Sinar-Kao S.A.). To expand its product palette and establish itself more as an international brand, Kao established, in 1971, a joint venture with the German company Beiersdorf for its brand Nivea and started selling the product under the Nivea-Kao Corporation. To keep expanding even further, Kao Group started to buy various brands like the Andrew Jergens Company and John Frieda Professional Haircare Inc. in the USA, Molton Brown in the U.K. and the Goldwell AG in Germany (Kao Corporation, 2020).

In the early 2000s, the Japanese cosmetics market was dominated by the big five: Shiseido, Kao, Kanebo, Albion (Kosé) and Pola-schrank — the company's strongest competitor being Shiseido. In order to stay competitive, the Kao Group was on the lookout for expanding the business. The area of cosmetics was of special interest since the market was constantly growing. In 2005, the cosmetics company Kanebo was listed for sale on the global market and the Kao Group saw a chance to acquire more cosmetics brands and to take the lead in the cosmetics industry. But, the acquisition of Kanebo was not an easy process. How did the sale work out in the end (Moulin, 2006)?

Kanebo History from Silk Production to Audit Scandal

Kanebo's roots are in silk production. Being founded in 1887, the company first started as a cotton trade company moving on to silk production. With its modernization of silk reeling, it made silk an important industry in Japan. In the 1930s, Kanebo's researchers found out that silk oil and other silk-derived components made the skin smoother. Their knowledge about silk was used to create the first beauty product, the silk-based soap Savon de Soei, a luxury good of French quality. The product sold out in Japan and the company planned to export to the European market, but had to hold plans in the face of World War I (Kanebo, 2019). With the knowledge the company gained on silk, it started to develop further cosmetic products in 1939, producing creams, lotions, pomades, face powders and shampoo. Through its groundbreaking research, Kanebo created its first anti-aging skin care products in the 60s, which started a Japan-wide trend. During this time, Kanebo expanded so fast that by 1961, its cosmetic products were sold in ten thousand cosmetics stores in Japan.

This was when the company entered the first Asian market. It started with sales in Hong Kong and expanded to Thailand, Taiwan, Indonesia, the Philippines and Singapore. Kanebo invested in its research laboratories and developed further products containing silk and Vitamin C. The entry to the European market only happened in 1979, almost 20 years after the start of the Asian expansion. It began by selling its brand JOSET at the department store Harrods in London, and sixteen European cities followed. In 1980, Kanebo Europe Cosmetics, Ltd. was launched. Kanebo Sensai introduced its new product, an ultra-luxurious anti-aging cream, to the European market and it became one of the most costly creams in the world and made Kanebo known for its outstanding quality. In the 90s and early 2000s, Kanebo introduced new brands to the global market. The growth of Kanebo then came to a sudden halt (Kanebo, 2019).

In 2004, Kanebo faced a huge accounting scandal which threatened the survival of the company. Kanebo admitted to overstating profits over several years. It was, up to that date, the biggest accounting scandal in Japan not involving a financial firm. Kanebo inflated its numbers from 1999 to March 2003, up to US$1.37 billion, while it in fact had big financial losses (BBC News, 2005). The shares of Kanebo plummeted after the accounting fraud was revealed and the listing of Kanebo's shares on the Tokyo Stock Exchange had to be reviewed; ultimately, the company was delisted from the stock market because of its negative net worth (Japan Times, 2005b). The management was made responsible for the scandal and had to face the consequences.

"All the directors of the board, including myself, feel seriously responsible for the current situation,"

—Takashi Hoashi, Chairman and President of Kanebo Ltd.

The chairman and president of Kanebo Ltd., Takashi Hoashi (68), formally announced his resignation and stepped down from his position in May. The company was faced with a more than 500 billion yen debt.

Before the scandal, Kanebo's cosmetics unit was financially the strongest of the company, accounting for 40% of the company's total revenue. The Kanebo cosmetics unit was separated from the Kanebo firm and the debt was transferred to Kanebo cosmetics because it had the strongest sales. Kao Group was interested in buying the new Kanebo Cosmetics company, but was not able to make the deal, so the Kanebo management decided to get funded. It restructured with the help of the Industrial

Revitalization Corporation of Japan, a government-affiliated organization, and the IRCJ would get the majority equity stake for its financial support of the company, mostly funded through taxpayer money (AFX European Focus, 2004). In July 2005, three executives and the former president were arrested for violating the law. The former president was sentenced to two years' imprisonment and the former vice president to one and a half years.

In 2005, it was again planned to sell the Kanebo Cosmetics company, and this time Kao was able to make the deal. In January 2006, Kanebo Cosmetics officially became part of the Kao Corporation. The manager of Kao Group, Motoki Ozakia, said he would let the brand continue operating under its name and not do any restructuring. Kao paid around 410 billion yen to acquire Kanebo Cosmetics and its patents and other rights (Japan Times, 2005a). Up until Kanebo's acquisition, Kao was mainly known as a detergent maker. Its new aim was to position itself as the main player on the cosmetics market (Jiji Press, 2006).

Kao's Growth plans for its Cosmetic Branch

After the acquisition, Kao was second on the market for cosmetics and toiletries with sales of ¥363 billion (US$3.07 billion), just falling a little behind Shiseido who had sales of ¥442 billion ($3.74 billion) in 2005. Kao became one of the leading cosmetics and skin care producers and operated in over 50 countries. Its brand portfolio contained over 14 brands, which produced and sold skin care products worldwide. But, the sale of the beauty care business started to stagger in 2012 — the sales of prestige cosmetics only rose by 0.1% in 2011. Kao's company-wide strategy for the upcoming year was to increase sales globally (Kao Corporation, 2012).

Kanebo Cosmetics president Masumi Natsusaka said Kanebo must think internationally since Japan's markets were almost saturated with only little growing potential left. He stated the following:

"I think the cosmetics industry has the potential to grow into one of Japan's leading industries, which can compete in the international market. Shiseido has already achieved this and, now, as [the second-largest Japanese cosmetics company], we need to do the same."

After Kao's acquisition of Kanebo Cosmetics, the management mainly focused on the domestic market to be able to compete with

Shiseido. Few investments since then were done to help grow the brand in overseas markets. Markets of special interest for Kanebo Cosmetics are China, Russia and Southeast Asia since they have the best growing potential. These markets are changing rapidly and offer a chance for new market entries. Even though the company wants to focus less on the US and European markets, because brands on these markets are already well established and growth in these markets takes time, it is still considering expanding into them more in the following years. Kanebo is already selling its products in 55 countries, but since the beginning it has not been following an international product strategy, and sales from international markets make up only 10% of sales, with China, Germany and Taiwan making the biggest profit. The goal for 2015 was to raise the percentage up to 15% and for 2020 to raise it to 30%. The Japanese competition is also starting to focus on the international market, but, unlike them, Kanebo wants to focus on its brands instead of growing through acquisitions. The management wants to focus on five specific brands out of Kanebo's vast portfolio: the prestige brands Sensai and Impress (Impress will be renamed to Kanebo), the skin care line Freshel, and the color cosmetic brands Lunasol and Kate. Most of the brands' products are already suitable for the international market. Still, some R&D is required. An example is products containing a lot of alcohol. While in Japan, consumers are used to it, in other countries, consumers prefer products with less alcohol. To cut costs, and to be closer to the target markets, Kanebo is considering starting to produce more in its China and France manufacturing facilities. Most of Kanebo's products are still produced in Japan and have high production costs. To be successful, Kanebo wants to focus on the needs of its international customers while continuing to grow on the Japanese market (Women Wear Daily, 2012).

The Skin-Whitening Scandal

Kanebo was able to grow under the Kao Group and started to develop new products and formulas until, in July 2013, it was again hit by a huge crisis regarding one of its products. On the 4th of July, Kanebo had to recall its first products. The reason was that many users started to report symptoms of skin damage. Around 9,000 people were affected; 2250 of them even reported serious damage. The skin damage was caused by various skin-whitening products from Kanebo and its subsidiaries Lissage Ltd. and

Équipe Ltd. The effects were depigmentation in various body areas the size of at least 5 cm. When Kanebo recalled its products, it said that it was only aware of 39 cases at that time. The president, Masumi Natsuka, issued an official apology to the customers who developed symptoms and stated that he was surprised by the high number of incidents. The skin-whitening products included the chemical 4-(4-hydroxyphenyl)-2-butanone, which was developed by Kanebo and named "Rhododenol", and was approved by the health ministry in 2008. Products with this ingredient had been sold since the same year with approximately 250,000 users over time. The products which were recalled were worth around ¥5 billion in sales on the home market and ¥1 billion on the overseas market. The company recommended for customers to consult medical facilities that were posted on the Japanese Dermatological Association to treat the symptoms (Japan Times, 2013). Long-term support to affected clients was planned which was to include skin condition checkups and advice on makeup application. A special committee at the Japanese Dermatology Association was set up on the 17th of July to investigate the cause and develop efficient treatments. There are no similar cases known from other brands, since the ingredient Rhodendol is only used by Kanebo brands. Over the following two months, more cases were made public.

During the investigations of the case, it was found that Kanebo started to recall its products too late into the process. One year earlier, in September 2012, there had already been reports stating the possibility of Kanebo's products causing the loss of skin pigmentation. Kanebo failed to investigate these cases and chose to hide cases of clients who complained about pigmentation issues. In a 1998 scientific paper, Professor Yoshiharu Fukuda of Yamaguchi University stated that three workers who were handling raspberry ketone at the chemical factory, a raw material for making 4HPB, first had signs of leukoderma around 1992, and that this matter was discussed by a panel of the health and welfare ministry's Pharmaceutical Affairs and Food Sanitation Council in 2007. 4HPB is produced by mixing raspberry ketone with hydrogen. It was suspected by the panel that raspberry ketone in reaction to sunlight can create skin changes. The Pharmaceuticals and Medical Device Agency, who were in charge of early screenings of the product, denied that such issues were known beforehand.

Kanebo received many indications that its products were causing leukoderma over the years, but chose to not investigate, hoping the issue would not become bigger. If Kanebo had chosen to act sooner, less people would have suffered and the company brand would not have had to face these huge losses. Kanebo's safety controls had failed and the internal corporate culture and communication channels were a major cause of this issue (Japan Times, 2013).

The Japanese Cosmetic Industry

In 2014, the Japanese cosmetics market was estimated at a volume of ¥2.331 trillion (20 billion euros) and therefore ranked as the second largest market worldwide. Over the last five years, the market was very stable and continued to grow every year. In Japan, women invest in cosmetics to keep their skin healthy in the long term and more men are starting to be part of the customer group. Almost half of the market sales are earned through skin care products, followed by makeup, hair, perfume and men's products. Skin care sales amounted to ¥1.07 trillion.

The premium cosmetics market in Japan has one of the biggest volumes of sales in the world and has been the main focus of Japanese cosmetic brands while neglecting the mass market. But, the mass market is still growing with each year and holds huge potential. In order to position themselves on the mass market, the big Japanese cosmetics players, Kanebo, Shiseido and Kose, had to start adapting their products to the low-cost skin care market. In this market, the competition is very strong because it is harder to keep customers. Shiseido has therefore created the brand "Senka", with products costing less than ¥1000 to be compatible on the market and to force the other brands to drop their prices to stay attractive for customers (Rannou, 2015).

The Market for Skin-Whitening Products

The market for skin-whitening products is growing each year. Light skin is still the beauty standard in the beauty industry and many female consumers want to achieve this look with skin care products. Companies fuel the demand by constantly bringing out new formulas with new ingredients which are supposed to be gentle and not damaging to the skin. The products reduce pigmentation, lighten discoloration, even skin tone and eliminate blemishes. Asia is one of the biggest markets for lightening products, but the market shares are also increasing in other parts of the world (Grand View Research, 2019, Skin Lightening Products Market Size, Share & Trends Analysis Report).

Aftermath

For Kanebo, this is one of the biggest scandals in the company's history, which threatened the survival of the brand. With thousands of customers suffering from leukoderma and starting to file for damage payments, the company had lost its trust from consumers. For the Kao group, this meant big financial losses. In total, ¥12.1 billion was attributed to the voluntary recall, which led to a decrease of ¥2.4 billion in gross profit. The cost for the return of the products to sellers was estimated at ¥9.7 billion (Kao Corporation, 2020).

Further costs are anticipated regarding compensation for medical treatment and costs for potential lawsuits. The image of Kanebo has suffered and might influence the sales for years to come. Because Kao Corporation owns more than 50 cosmetics brands, there is a potential risk that the skin-whitening scandal might tarnish the image of other brands in the Kao Group brand portfolio and decrease sales for the following years because customers fear further issues. On the contrary, the chances are low that the Kanebo scandal is associated with Kao or any other brands under Kao. Few people in Japan are aware of the connections between different cosmetic brands and the conglomerate structure is even less known in other countries. Kao Group needs to develop a strategy to be able to manage its huge brand portfolio. While its many brands are an advantage in Japan, this creates a problem overseas that Kao cannot form a strong brand image. Each brand is known just for itself and the brands cannot profit from each other's popularity. For the future, Kao Group needs to create a marketing strategy to present itself as one strong brand in order to be successful on the global cosmetics market and secure its position as one of the biggest cosmetic companies in the world.

Questions

1. How can Kanebo regain the trust of its customers and market new products in the future?
2. Which processes and safety procedures need to be developed in the Kao Group that such cases do not happen again with other brands?
3. Which strategy should Kao pursue to secure its growth on the international cosmetics market?

References

AFX European Focus (2004). Japan's Kanebo president to resign over management failure — Report.

BBC News (2005). Cosmetic firm in accounts scandal. http://news.bbc.co.uk/2/hi/business/4439615.stm. (Accessed on January 2, 2020).

Grand View Research (2019). Skin Lightening Products Market Size, Share & Trends Analysis Report By Product (Cream, Cleanser, Mask), By Nature (Synthetic, Natural, Organic), By Region, And Segment Forecasts, 2019–2025, https://www.grandviewresearch.com/industry-analysis/skin-lightening-products-market. (Accessed on December 1, 2020).

Japan Times (2005a). Kao lets Kanebo live one. https://www.japantimes.co.jp/news/2005/12/17/national/kao-lets-kanebo-live-on/#.XdIjYK_grX4. (Accessed on January 13, 2020).

Japan Times (2005b). TSE to delist Kanebo over accounting scandal. https://tinyurl.com/y8ztywgg. (Accessed on January 13, 2020).

Japan Times (2013). 2,250 users of Kanebo skin-whitening products report serious symptoms. https://www.japantimes.co.jp/news/2013/07/23/business/corporate-business/2250-users-of-kanebo-skin-whitening-products-report-serious-symptoms/. (Accessed on January 16, 2020).

Japan Times (2013). Kanebo's costly scandal. https://www.japantimes.co.jp/opinion/2013/09/16/editorials/kanebos-costly-scandal/#.XdFHmq_grX4. (Accessed on January 3, 2020).

Jiji Press (2006). Tokyo Report: 'Big Two' Cosmetics Makers Intensify Rivalry.

Kanebo (2019). Our History. https://www.kanebo.com/history/. (Accessed on December 1, 2020).

Kanebo (2019). A beautiful beginning: The gift of silk. https://www.kanebo.com/history/column/gift-of-silk/. (Accessed on December 1, 2020).

Kao Corporation (2020). https://www.kao.com/emea/en/. (Accessed November 12, 2020).

Moulin, C. (2006). Showdown: Japanese brands. International Cosmetic News, Regional Report, Vol. 87.

Rannou, E. (2015). Japanese Cosmetics Market Obstacles and Opportunities for European SMEs. https://www.eu-japan.eu/sites/default/files/publications/docs/japanesecosmetics_final.pdf. (Accessed on January 13, 2020).

Women's Wear Daily (2012). Kanebo's Overseas Growth Plan, Vol. 204.

© 2021 World Scientific Publishing Company
https://doi.org/10.1142/9789811231032_0007

Case 7

Shiseido — Traditions and Restructuring the Hard Way

Le Ha My

Introduction

Japanese cosmetics corporation Shiseido is one of the oldest cosmetics companies in Japan, dating back to the 19th century. Its main cosmetics brand, SHISEIDO Ginza Tokyo, which advertises itself as a perfect combination of West and East, can be found in most department stores across Japan and neighboring countries such as South Korea, China, Hong Kong and Vietnam. The company was also one of the first Japanese companies to expand abroad when it entered the Southeast Asian market as early as 1932, and started putting more emphasis on foreign markets in the 1970s. Ever since, the company has been enjoying success as a global company with a great share of its revenue coming from outside Japan. In fact, currently, its revenue outside Japan accounts for 60% of the company's total revenue. Needless to say, sales in both the domestic and global markets are equally important for the company.

In 2019, Shiseido corporation, which nowadays consists of many different cosmetics brands, was ranked the Number 1 cosmetics brand in Asia by sales. This is believed to be attributed to the company's vigorous acquisition strategy, constant expansion to foreign markets and its proper segmentation strategy.

The company had for a long time enjoyed half of its sales coming from the domestic market. However, with an aging population and an

81

unchanging Japanese cosmetics market, the company recognized that now, more than ever, venturing out of Japan was important and being the top cosmetics manufacturer only in Asia was not enough. Hence, the company has been putting more emphasis on developing its image in Western countries. In order to attain this, in 2010, the company acquired a growing cosmetics manufacturer in the USA to introduce itself to the market. While an acquisition strategy previously seemed an effective way to expand, this time the strategy backfired due to cultural differences and poor international management, causing the company to claim losses for many consecutive years. As a result, despite the determination and success in the Asia Pacific region, both the European and US markets are still lagging behind.

In response to the crisis, new CEO Masahi Uotani was appointed, hoping to bring radical changes and optimism. However, the question as to whether or not Shiseido gets back on its feet still remains.

Anti-Aging Empire

Being one of the oldest cosmetics companies in the world, Shiseido was founded in 1872 as a Western pharmaceutical company. It opened its first cosmetics shop in 1916, marking the company's reorientation to the cosmetics industry. From the beginning, Shiseido positioned itself with the following five key points: (1) Creativity and Innovation in all its product offerings; (2) unique blend of the oriental mystique and sensitivity with Western fashion values; (3) application of clinically tested formulae to enhance skin care and beauty; (4) customization of offerings to different markets; and (5) strong distribution strategy.

Overall, Shiseido's success is brought about by commitment to answering the needs of its customers thanks to high product quality, regular technological innovations, careful segmentation, as well as the broad geographical area in which Shiseido's products are being produced and distributed. Throughout its history, the company was able to gain trust from its customers.

Brand Management

In order to understand customers' needs, the company divided its customers into different segments based on age and life stage. In order to tackle different groups and guarantee the best customized products answering to each group's needs, the corporation had different brands for different segments, according to Sihavong and Surono (1999), cited in Leelapanyalert *et al.* (2015). For instance, two well-known brands under Shiseido umbrella are SHISEIDO and Za SHISEIDO (now known as SHISEIDO Ginza Tokyo) is a high-end cosmetics brand, well known for its whitening and anti-aging products, and is only sold in luxurious department stores such as Daimaru, Isetan and Takashimaya. The brand aims at answering the needs of middle-aged women with a stable income, while it also attracts other cosmetics lovers with its innovations in the beauty industry. Za, on the contrary, has a very different image despite being owned by the same corporation, SHISEIDO. Za lures customers in with its convenience and low prices. The brand comes across as trendy, young and energetic, and it can be found in most drug stores, making it accessible to the wider public and more convenient to purchase. Regarding the products, Za also offers more variations in terms of colors (especially products like eyeliners, eyeshadows and blushes), aligning with younger consumers' need to experiment and try out new things, many of whom are still unsure of what looks they are striving for. This can only be allowed with Za because of the low cost of the products, making it affordable for customers to buy more colors and be able to change around their looks whenever they please. With youngsters in their late teens and early 20s being the target, this is a suitable strategy because it allows the customers to constantly change their style while also experimenting with new looks.

Using a segmentation strategy, the company was able to tackle different groups of customers by having a wide range of products from quality to price, allowing all groups of consumers to be able to find a suitable product answering to their needs and their budget. Thanks to this strategy, the company was also able to maintain the luxurious perception of its main brand SHISEIDO Ginza Tokyo. Moreover, when the customers grow older or start having a need for more luxurious products, they can easily switch from Za to SHISEIDO Ginza Tokyo because the customers were already used to consistent quality and products provided by Za. That way, Shiseido not only provides products of all ranges but it also gets the customers before the customers even develop the need for high-end cosmetics products.

Global Distribution

In addition to the segmentation strategy, the company paid close attention to geographical distribution. Despite being a traditional Japanese company, Shiseido started venturing out of its domestic market as early as 1932 when it was exporting its products to the Southeast Asian market. In 1957, the company began sales in Taiwan, which was quickly followed by penetration of the Singapore and the Hong Kong markets. The corporation started putting more emphasis on foreign markets in the 1970s and soon found itself in quite a successful position when around half of the company's revenue came from overseas markets. Nowadays, the company is present in over 120 countries and regions and was named Number 1 in WWD BEAUTY INC's "The 2018 Beauty Top 100" list for Japanese and Asian manufacturers based on annual sales in April 2019, according to the official website.

Being one of the first Asian brands to venture outside Asia, Shiseido leveraged its Asian image as it advertises itself as "truly Asian", which can be seen through its packaging, advertisements, products and most recently by how its main brand Shiseido has been rebranded to *SHISEIDO Ginza Tokyo*. "Ginza" and "Tokyo" are two most familiar names when Japan is mentioned. Not only does it represent the cosmetics brand's origins but "Ginza" is also commonly known to be a luxurious high-end and sophisticated shopping area that attracts successful and well-off women who are usually always on top of fashion trends.

As well as being one of the first Japanese companies to venture outside Japan, Shiseido was also one of the first Asian companies to grow through the acquisition strategy, allowing the company to easily enter a foreign market with customers' acceptance. The customers' acceptance is seen more with Shiseido than other companies because it openly communicates the companies it acquires. For instance, many brands that Shiseido owns also have "Shiseido" written on their packaging.

Nowadays, Shiseido not only owns brands for cosmetics products but also provides other beautifying products such as vitamins, sun cream and makeup tools such as brushes.

Losses

Over the course of over 100 years, the company has been able to build its own cosmetics empire as it became one of the most popular cosmetics manufacturers not only in Japan but also in several neighboring countries, especially in East Asia. However, due to poor management, inability to quickly adjust to consumers' needs as well as other factors, this empire started "losing its crown". As the sales were quickly dropping both domestically and internationally, losses had to be declared, and the company's image was no longer attractive to consumers.

For the five years following the global financial crisis from 2008 to 2013, it was apparent that the size of the cosmetics market in Japan did not grow, staying at around 2.250 trillion yen, as people gave preference to other needs. Another reason why the Japanese cosmetics market witnessed a slow change was the growing proportion of the elderly population. Due to the overall shrinking population, the market competition became even more fierce as most companies were under pressure to report growth and increased profit annually. Under these conditions, Shiseido's market share dropped from a little over 18% in the first quarter of 2008 to around 15% in the first quarter of 2013, according to numbers reported by Shiseido (2013). In other words, Shiseido was losing touch with its domestic market and started losing shares. This, for the company, was a major problem, not only because the domestic sales still accounted for about half of the company's revenue but also because the Japanese were known to be among the most prolific consumers of cosmetics. In effect, the company was losing its position as the number 1 cosmetics manufacturer in Japan.

Domestic sales have fallen or stagnated each year since 2010 due to a lack of response to the growing lower-priced cosmetics demand, which resulted from the global financial crisis. According to Shiseido's annual report in 2013, from 2009 to 2013, domestic sales saw a major dip. More specifically, in 2009, domestic sales accounted for 428.3 billion yen, while in 2013, this number was down to 373.2 billion yen (Shiseido, 2013). The corporation also underperformed compared to its closest domestic rival, Kao Corporation, which owns Kanebo Cosmetics and household goods, according to the Financial Times (2015). Hence, it was even more important at this point for the company to start putting more emphasis on the global market, in addition to strengthening its position within Japan.

While the makeup giant's way out was supposed to be markets outside Japan, the cosmetics manufacturer did not perform any better as it was facing many challenges there as well. The first problem the company had to solve was struggles in one of its most profitable markets outside Japan — China. One of Shiseido's biggest strengths is the power of its brand name Shiseido, which has for a long time been associated with innovation, top quality and consistent quality. However, with anti-Japan sentiment in China in 2013, the company's brand name became a burden and obstacle, rather than a strength. As a result, Shiseido witnessed a major dip in sales due to customers' refusal to buy Japanese products. Its profit in China in 2013 only totaled 5 billion yen, 60% less than the year before. In addition to losing its grasp on the Chinese market, Shiseido was also left far behind by other major cosmetics companies including France's L'Oreal Group and Estee Lauder of the US, as Chinese customers were seeking to replace their Japanese products (Nikkei Asian Review, 2014).

With a steady decline in domestic market share, the company implemented cost-cutting measures to boost profits, which also resulted in decreased allocation for R&D and marketing in the budget. According to Jun Aoki, Director and Executive Corporate Officer of Shiseido, most customers viewed Shiseido as reliable but not dynamic.

"These past few years, Shiseido seemed to lose sight of their own path," Aoki said in an interview with CELM Asia, addressing the company's lack of innovation and adaptability in its products due to the decreased investment in developing new products.

"Japanese companies have a high level of technology but a bit of weakness in marketing because you can see that in Japan it's basically one language and one similar culture," Masahi said in an interview with Financial Times (Scheherazade, 2015), further emphasizing the trouble the makeup conglomerate was going through.

Struggling in the Asian Pacific market, which the company considered its major playing field, Shiseido did not perform much better in the US and European markets. Differences in national culture, laws, regulations and corporate practices of the United States and Europe, which from now on will be referred to as "the West", were a major challenge for Shiseido.

Failed Acquisition Strategy

To expand into the global market, Shiseido mostly relied on acquisition strategy, which allowed the company to familiarize itself with the market due to major cultural differences. The acquisition of international cosmetics brands like NARs and Bare Escentuals allowed the company to raise consumers' perceptions and familiarize themselves with Shiseido. This is considered to be a safe choice because it would have been difficult to introduce a new brand into the market due to difference in lifestyle, brand image and customers' perceptions of Japanese consumers and those in the Western countries. Moreover, the company has been implementing the acquisition strategy to boost growth for many years, so the management board was not hesitant when the opportunity to acquire growing American makeup company Bare Escentuals, most known for its makeup line Bare Minerals, came up.

However, difference in culture not only posed challenges during the merging and acquisition process of Bare Escentuals but also turned out to be one of Shiseido's major failures, dragging down the company's annual report in 2013, forcing the company to post an extraordinary loss of 14.7 billion yen for the fiscal year 2013 (Shiseido, 2013). The acquisition started out full of potential when Shiseido hoped to gain more popularity and successfully penetrate the US market — a mission remaining unaccomplished for the past 10 years. After the acquisition, Bare Escentuals' sales slowed down and resulted in an overall loss in the fiscal year 2013.

Globally, Shiseido is one of the best-known names in cosmetics with brands such as Elixir, Maquillage and the top-of-the-range Clé de Peau. Shiseido was ranked fourth biggest company globally in 2010, but dropped down to fifth in 2015, according to CELM Asia. Its 2% share of the beauty market is not far off Estée Lauder's 3%, but well below L'Oréal, which has 9.7%, according to Bernstein Research (Daneshku, 2015).

Management Issues

In addition to the difference in culture during acquisition, the company's traditional management was another cause of the company's losses in the early 2010s. While the company was a global name and known as a modern Japanese company, it was not until 2014 that it stubbornly held onto its traditional Japanese management style with managers, especially top managers, with people always being groomed from the inside. This is a tradition commonly practiced in Japanese companies, with Shiseido being no exception ever since it was set up in 1872 as Japan's first Western-style pharmacy.

Japanese traditional management can be defined using four main characteristics: (1) Lifetime employment; (2) seniority system of compensation; (3) Japanese traditional system of decision making; and (4) company trade unions. In addition to these four main characteristics, there are others such as in-house training of managers, extensive use of quality control methods, emphasis on creating harmonious relations among workers, and so on (Rudy, 2008).

As a result of these characteristics, in Japanese traditional management styles, employees usually do not have a specified position and rather rotate jobs when they are working in the company. Employees remain loyal to the company and are considered to be a flexible work force that can go from one department to another due to the lack of specification in their labor contract. Because of the lifetime employment system, it is commonly found that employees stay in one company for their whole life. In other words, it is of extreme rarity that individuals are hired mid-career into other companies. With the seniority system as a traditional feature of Japanese approach, the internal career promotion system is based on the age of employees and time spent within a company. Managers in a traditional Japanese company tend to be selected internally, so usually they do not know any practices outside the company they work for. Lastly, in a Japanese company, there are no specific guidelines passed down by top management and no specific responsibilities that are borne by a sole employee. All decisions, besides the most routine ones, have to be submitted and approved by top managers and all the responsibility is shared (Rudy, 2008).

As mentioned above, Shiseido had for a long time been loyal to the traditional Japanese management system, which meant that no managers were brought from outside and usually were seniors groomed by the company and who had spent their whole life working for Shiseido. This changed in 2011 when Shiseido's then president Maeda Shinzo stepped aside to allow his close aide Suekawa Hisayuki to become CEO of the famed makeup corporation. Under Suekawa's management, the company ran into great losses and slumped in performance. This was partially because of Suekawa's lack of understanding of marketing and the change of customers' needs, which could be expected, considering the fact that he had worked in Shiseido for most of his life. Suekawa's reign lasted two years before he resigned citing poor health. Shiseido desperately looked for another successor in the company to replace the retired CEO, but had not been able to find one, which for the company was a major problem. Stubbornly holding onto its own traditional ways, it was rather difficult for the board to accept the fact that it had to look outside the company for a suitable candidate for this position and that an "outsider" would have to be trusted to get the company out of the great losses and tricky situation it was in (Kazuo, 2014).

New Breeze

In April 2014, 60-year-old Masahi Uotani, former employee at Coca-Cola Japan, was appointed first CEO brought in from outside the company. Masahi said he could feel "a strong sense of crisis when I considered Shiseido's current circumstances." Appointing Masahi as the first outsider CEO not only points out the board's acknowledgement for the need to change but also the dire situation Shiseido found itself in. Most importantly, it also showed the need for specialization as the board picked a former marketing manager of Coca-Cola.

Even Masahi, a Japanese citizen, had to point to "the flip side" of Japanese culture after his promotion, which he was able to do thanks to his experience studying abroad and working for a Western company for many years. He claimed that the current practice of a seniority order was one of the main drawbacks in the management of human resources at Shiseido and that despite the company's modern and global image, this way of doing things still prevailed.

"Even if you are good, you have to wait. In the western management style, it doesn't matter what age you are, whether you are a man or a woman," Masahi said, hinting that there was still an inclination toward male managers and the company's demographics were lacking in diversity with female employees still being at a disadvantage. He also believed it was because of this lack of diversity that the company was struggling to adapt to different cultures, markets and quickly changing needs of consumers, resulting in decreasing sales, failure to become a major cosmetics player in Western countries and a troublesome merger with Bare Escentuals.

Another problem the company was facing was employees' traditional and old-fashioned mindset, where many managers, especially corporate officers, believed they have reached the highest position in their lifetime career. With that, they stopped challenging themselves with the missions that have a higher degree of difficulty, preventing the company from striving overall.

In other words, Shiseido was having a major crisis where it was having both internal and external problems. The company was outperformed by its rivals both domestically and globally. The company's acquisition of Bare Escentuals caused major losses, and while sales were dropping, the shrinking beauty market in Japan was not an advantage either.

The management proved to be inadequate to deal with the current crisis. The traditional Japanese way of home-growing their managers

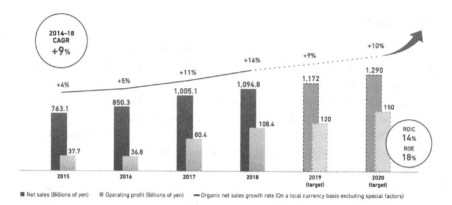

Figure 1.   Shiseido's expected growth for 2019 and 2020 (Shiseido, 2018).

backfired with the fast-changing market and the crisis the company was facing. Employees' traditional mindset of respecting the elderly also did not help, as most of the managers were the ones who had been working in the company long enough, rather than those who deserved the position.

Overall, all of these problems arose at once, alerting the company of the need for radical change or expected death of a 100-year-old Japanese cosmetics brand. Fortunately, as the former CEO Suekawa Hisayuki stepped down, the company realized the need for radical change rather than holding on to traditional ways, only to experience failure at the end of the road. With that, radical change quickly began with new a CEO stepping up to keep Shiseido not just afloat but on top (Figure 1).

"VISION 2020"

The first moves toward the change began in April 2014 when the board appointed Masahi Uotani as the new CEO, with his mission being clear: winning back the domestic cosmetics market share while also finding a way to conquer the US market, where the company owns two well-known cosmetics brands, NARS and Bare Escentuals.

Masahi Uotani brought high hopes with his radical changes and Western way of thinking, due to his excellent English and time spent in the USA, attaining his MBA degree at Columbia University. Additionally, he had spent most of his life working for US consumer goods companies located in Japan (Daneshkhu, 2015).

While the Shiseido board highlighted his "experience in the global business field" and his "high level of marketing ability" upon the appointment of his new role, Uotani admitted to "a bit of hesitation" when he was offered the job.

"There is a big difference between global companies and the Japanese company in terms of culture, in terms of the way you do the business," he admitted in an interview with Financial Times (2015).

Makeover of Shiseido

In December 2015, the *VISION 2020* strategy was created in order to tackle two main challenges the company was facing at the time, preventing growth and increase in profits. First, the company was no longer relevant to what consumers needed. Second, with the decrease in marketing and research and development, the company was unable to adapt to the ever-changing market (Heide and Gontarz, 2016). According to Heide and Gontarz's (2016) citation of Shiseido (2015), the strategy also set out several targets including the following: (1) becoming a company benefiting the society and needed by the consumers globally; (2) becoming a youthful company full of energy; (3) appealing to the young consumers; and (4) becoming a multicultural company that promotes and is suitable for diverse cultures. Overall, the company's biggest goal in this plan was to rebrand itself in order to be viewed differently by the consumers.

VISION 2020 consists of two three-year plans, with the first being "Restructure the Business Foundation" and the second being "New Strategy to Accelerate Growth". In the first three-year plan, the company was focused on enhancing brands, increasing marketing and R&D investment, organizational and personnel reform, and strengthening some of the Asian markets, which is expected to become a strong foundation for the growth boost expected to be seen in the latter half of the *Vision 2020* strategy (Shiseido, 2015).

Over 100 products of its main brand *SHISEIDO* were discontinued. The company itself also went through a radical rebranding process with many new products being introduced in addition to new simplified and modern packaging (Brennan, 2018), as well as logo and brand name, in order to change the way it is perceived by the consumers. Popular logo *SHISEIDO* has been replaced with *SHISEIDO Ginza Tokyo* to further accentuate its origins from Japan. The company explains that the idea aims at "expressing elements of contemporary Japan fundamental to

Shiseido from a global perspective". While there was more focus put on the company's Asian origins, the brand still remained "Western" by introducing a new collection of over 22 products designed in New York City. It was hoped that the new image would attract younger consumers, especially those in their 20s and 30s. With this new incentive, Shiseido aimed to grow sales by 20% by 2020 (Du and Takahashi, 2018).

Another big goal that Shiseido was trying to attain in *VISION 2020* was tackling the travel retail market, which was experiencing a boom due to an increase in international traveling worldwide. The travel retail market is the market for visitors and tourists, which also includes airport retail. Shiseido was setting this to be its major milestone for *VISION 2020* (Ng, 2019). In order to attain that, the company also created a unified travel retail division named Shiseido Travel Retail, including brands that are believed to appeal to traveling consumers (Moodie, 2016). Many changes have been made to the products of several brands that aim at attracting target customers in the travel retail market. For instance, SHISEIDO Ginza Tokyo's new product range was simplified to four categories, making it easier for consumers to navigate, especially considering the time-constrained environment of travel retail (Austin, 2015). The company also started putting emphasis on enhancing its prestige premium brands that are famed for being manufactured in Japan, which include Elixir, Anessa and Laura Mercier, among others, which have for a long time been loved by traveling consumers, especially in Asia (Rozario, 2019).

In 2019, the company also unveiled its new global headquarters in Singapore, believing that the new office, as well as the office's location, will best boost the Shiseido Travel Retail segment in the Asia-Pacific region, which also has offices in Paris, Miami, Dubai, Hong Kong and Shanghai (Ng, 2019).

Further Investment in the Future

After the company's major setback in the late 2000s and early 2010s, Shiseido tried to stay on top of the game and not fall behind its competitors. In order to once again become a trend-setting and innovating makeup company that is not only trustworthy but also innovative, Shiseido recognizes the importance of innovation. Hence, Shiseido started its focus on innovation with its major investment into building a Global Innovation Centre (GIC) in Yokohama, Japan, on top of investments into a travel retail headquarters in Singapore, both of which were opened in 2019.

With the ever-changing consumers' needs and dynamics, the company also recognizes fast change in the technology that can be implemented in the cosmetics market. Hence, Shiseido, once again, relies on acquisition strategy to stay up-to-date and ahead of the times when it comes to technology. On January 2018, Shiseido disclosed the acquisition of the R&D team and other assets of Olivo Laboratories, a start-up specializing in artificial skin technology that is based in Watertown, Massachusetts, close to Harvard and MIT.

It can also be seen that Shiseido does not want to lag behind when it comes to digital technology. In 2017, Shiseido made the headlines with the acquisition of a Silicon Valley firm that allowed using smartphones to sense skin color and use that data to customize makeup products. This technology perfectly matches Shiseido's emphasis of providing each customer with a different experience. The acquisition was followed by the company's announcement in July 2019 of its new strategy of "Total solutions using technology", which is also a part of its long-term plan, *VISION 2020*.

The company also bought AI-developing start-up Giaran in 2017, promising a future where customers can apply makeup virtually so they can see how they look before making purchases.

"Our customers' needs and demands are ever-changing. We need to be a step ahead of our customers, which means anticipating their needs, delivering and providing them with value-added brand experiences wherever they are," explained Pranary Mehra, vice president of digital and e-commerce at Shiseido Asia Pacific, in response to Shiseido's shift to become more digitally minded, starting with the acquisition of several potential start-ups in technology.

The company continues to grow through partnership and acquisitions as Mehra explained; Shiseido partnered with Alibaba Group in China and Southeast Asia for e-commerce efficiency.

As for the future, Shiseido acknowledges the importance of tech development. The company intends to boost its R&D staff to 1,500 in 2020, up from 1,000 in 2014. With this change, Shiseido hopes to once again lure its customers in with the company's innovativeness like it has been known for many years (Einhorn and Du, 2018).

Shake up the Human Resources

VISION 2020 for Masahi Uotani was not just about profit and numbers. He was also determined to change the company's dynamics and

Figure 2.   Percentage of female leaders working at Shiseido both in Japan and in the company's overseas offices (Shiseido, 2018).

demographics. According to his interview with Leader's Voice Nikkei, he admitted that Shiseido's demographics were lacking diversity in all aspects, with the most noticeable one being the lack of female managers, which is also one of the most typical characteristics of a traditional Japanese management system (Figure 2) (Nikkei Asian Review, 2017).

"When I worked for Coca Cola Japan, my boss was a younger American woman. Many Japanese may have found it difficult or uncomfortable to work in such a situation, but it was completely unremarkable in a company where diversity was the norm," Masahi said in the interview, pointing out the importance of having a more diverse workforce (Daneshkhu, 2015).

With this mindset, it was not surprising that one of Masahi's first decisions was to shake up the way brand managers work. Instead of developing products then handing over to a separate team, he made them responsible for selling as well. He abolished sales quotas in favor of broader "evaluation targets" tilted toward customer satisfaction measures and introduced more merit-based promotions aimed at motivating younger employees.

It was apparent that the company's way of working was becoming passive, dull and was lacking diversity, as well as innovation under the traditional management before Masahi Uotani came to Shiseido. In order to change this, Masahi introduced a more diverse and contemporary atmosphere to the company, starting with empowering the female workforce. One of the steps toward this was officially announcing the ratio and the number of female employees in the company on Shiseido's official website.

Masahi put forward educational programs for the employees and encouraged them to participate in the trainings, in addition to changing the company's communication language to English. Shiseido launched a digital academy for over 2,500 employees in six regions to equip its workforce with necessary knowledge in the digital age (Cameron, 2018).

"We are committed to investing in our people and by creating an inspirational environment, we aim to lift the energy and mood of our team," Shiseido Travel Retail President and CEO Philippe Lesné said in an interview (Ng, 2019).

Future Challenges

While the strategy is promising, whether Shiseido reaches its goals is still questionable. According to the company, the best way to boost sales in Europe, which remains one of the main weaknesses of the Japanese conglomerate, is to have a younger brand image. However, the company's current success in East Asia, and especially Japan, is due to its traditional values and consistency in the quality and image. Whether this strategy will lure the European consumers and Asian ones is still a question.

Additionally, while VISION 2020 is greatly defined by the radical change in technology and diversity, the middle management presents an obstacle. It is difficult to embrace diversity if managers do not understand it, especially when the management can be more traditional like in most Japanese companies' cases. Just as water only flows downward, change will only flow through to the rest of the company if you change the top level. It is important to skillfully utilize the corporate hierarchy to encourage growth.

Recently, CEO Masahi Uotani has gone public about the firm's loss of around 40 billion to 50 billion yen due to product shortages. Hence, the company is still waiting to resolve its supply chain issues. Much hope is held for the new Kyushu Fukuoka factory that is scheduled to begin operation in 2021 (Lim, 2019), but whether it can truly solve the company's supply chain problems is still a question.

Moreover, while the sales have increased, the new CEO also made several costly and radical acquisitions of tech companies that have not yet seemed to have immediate results. While managers of the makeup giant believe such movements are necessary to keep up with the needs of consumers, only about 16% of purchases in 2013 were done online.

Questions

1. Was rebranding the only option Shiseido had? What other strategies would be suitable for the abovementioned crisis.
2. How can Shiseido win Japan's market now that it is shrinking?
3. What else can be done to further boost the profitability and appeal of Shiseido in the travel retail market?
4. Shiseido is currently investing in Artificial Intelligence and Digitalization. Is it needed (and profitable) for a makeup company?
5. The Japanese top management system proved to be inefficient. However, should the way of recruiting change as well, so that employees would have a specified working position in the recruiting process rather than allowing freedom to change and explore several positions in the company?

References

Austin, C. (2015). Shiseido updates its global identity with major rebranding exercise. *The moodle report.* https://www.moodiedavittreport.com/shiseido-updates-its-global-identity-with-major-rebranding-exercise/ (Accessed on December 5, 2019).

Brennan, N. (2018). Your first look at an all new Shiseido. *ELLE Canada.* Available at: https://www.ellecanada.com/beauty/makeup-and-nails/your-first-look-at-an-all-new-shiseido (Accessed on November 17, 2019).

Cameron, N. (2018). A look into Shiseido's digital transformation ambitions. *CMO.* https://www.cmo.com.au/article/print/642410/look-into-shiseido-digital-transformation-ambitions/ (Accessed on December 4, 2019).

CNBC Online. (2018). CNBC Transcript: Masahiko Uotani, CEO, Shiseido. CNBC, 16 November [Online]. Available at: https://www.cnbc.com/2018/11/16/cnbc-transcript-masahiko-uotani-ceo-shiseido.html (Accessed on 16 November 2019).

Daneshku, S. (2015). A makeover using Western techniques. Gulf News, 26 January. https://www.pressreader.com/uae/gulf-news/20150126/282561606575842 (Accessed on November 23, 2019).

Du, L. and Takahashi, M. (2018). 146-year-old cosmetics firm Shiseido gets makeover to woo millenial buyers. *Bloomberg,* 2 August. https://tinyurl.com/ycttq86a (Accessed on November 17, 2019).

Einhorn, B. and Du, L. (2018). Beauty giant Shiseido snaps up technology start-ups to draw young shoppers. Bloomberg, 18 April [Online]. Available at:

https://www.japantimes.co.jp/news/2018/04/18/business/corporate-business/beauty-giant-shiseido-snaps-technology-startups-draw-young-shoppers/ (Accessed on December 5, 2019).

Heide, M. and Gontarz, K. M. (2016). *A brand positioning strategy recommendation for and Asian cosmetics giant: Shiseido in Western and Central Europe.* Master thesis. Copenhagen Business School. https://www.coursehero.com/file/52768702/Marleen-ter-Heidepdf/ (Accessed on November 23, 2019).

Kazuo, M. (2014). Japanese companies looking outside the fold for executive talent', *Nippon.com*, 14 August. https://www.nippon.com/en/currents/d00134/japanese-companies-looking-outside-the-fold-for-executive-talent.html (December 16, 2019).

Leelapanyalert, K. *et al.* (2015). Shiseido Group: The Turning Points, Challenges and Future Opportunities. *Academy of Asian Business Review.* ISSN: 2384-3454/15.

Lim, A. (2019). Shiseido's supply chain struggle: CEO estimates product hortages led to $450m sales loss. CosmeticsDesign-Asia.com, 19 February. https://tinyurl.com/ycd2dncd. (Accessed on December 4, 2019).

McEleny, C. (2019). How Shiseido is planning to thrive as consumers change the way they buy beauty products. www.thedrum.com, 9 July [Online] Available at: https://www.thedrum.com/news/2019/07/09/how-shiseido-planning-thrive-consumers-change-the-way-they-buy-beauty-products (Accessed on December 4, 2019).

Ng, M. (2019). Shiseido Travel Retail Gets Future-Ready With New Global Headquarters: Interview. *Jing Daily*, 1 February. https://jingdaily.com/shiseido-travel-retail/ (Accessed on January 20, 2019).

Nikkei Asian Review (2014). Shiseido hoping 'stealth' strategy in China more than cosmetic', 13 February. https://asia.nikkei.com/Business/Shiseido-hoping-stealth-strategy-in-China-more-than-cosmetic2 (Accessed on December 4, 2019).

Nikkei Asian Review (2017). Japan's Shiseido aims for 40% female management by 2020', 6 January. https://asia.nikkei.com/Business/Japan-s-Shiseido-aims-for-40-female-management-by-2020 (Accessed on December 4, 2019).

Rozario, K. (2019). Shiseido puts global focus on Elixir and Anessa brands as travel retail booms. *The Moodie Davitt Report,* 2 December. https://www.moodiedavittreport.com/shiseido-puts-global-focus-on-elixir-and-anessa-brands-as-travel-retail-booms/ (Accessed on January 15, 2019).

Rudy, J. (2008). *Traditional Japanese Management.* November. https://www.sjf.tuke.sk/transferinovacii/pages/archiv/transfer/11-2008/pdf/34-38.pdf (Accessed on December 21, 2019).

Scheherazade, D. (2015). Masahiko Uotani, Shiseido CEO: from Coke to cosmetics', *Financial Times,* 11 January. https://www.ft.com/content/bd7b83f2-9296-11e4-a1fd-00144feabdc0 (Accessed on November 16, 2019).

Shiseido (2013). Annual report. https://s3-us-west-2.amazonaws.com/ungc-production/attachments/32071/original/Annual%20Report%202013%20e%20.pdf?1378364719 (Accessed on November 18, 2019).

Shiseido (2014). Annual report. https://s3-us-west-2.amazonaws.com/ungc-production/attachments/cop_2014/105751/original/Annual_Report_2014_e.pdf?1409814345 (Accessed on November 18, 2019).

Shiseido (2015). Annual report. https://corp.shiseido.com/en/ir/library/annual/pdf/2015/anu00001.pdf(Accessed on November 18, 2019).

Shiseido (2018). Annual report [Online]. Available at: https://corp.shiseido.com/report/en/2018/ (Accessed on November 18, 2019).

© 2021 World Scientific Publishing Company
https://doi.org/10.1142/9789811231032_0008

Case 8

Sony and its Most Profitable Division — PlayStation

Pavel Burak

Introduction

This case study aims to analyze the development of Game & Network Services (G&NS) and how in just over two decades it has become by far the most profitable division for Sony. Sony is a huge corporation to cover in detail, so this case study will focus only on one of the many segments that Sony specializes in. This sector in itself is a great example of vertical integration since Sony produces the hardware such as the consoles and also supplies the aforementioned hardware with its own services and software as well as making deals with outside publishers and occasionally acquiring them, which is a perfect example.

Sony Corporation

Sony is a Japanese Conglomerate which is widely known internationally for the high-quality electronics it produces. Founded in 1946 as Tokyo Tsushin Kogyo and in 1958 renamed as Sony for easier integration into overseas markets, according to Ingham (2018), Sony is the biggest music company in the world. It is also the largest video game console business as well as one of the largest video game publishing businesses. In addition, it is a leader in consumer- and professional-grade electronics while also leading in film and television entertainment (Sony, 2020). Sony also has a very profitable finance division which until recently was the main profit maker for Sony, which is evident in its corporate reports leading up to 2017. Finally, Sony is currently ranked just outside the top 100 companies at 116 (Fortune, 2020), ranking at 97 at the end of 2018 and even having been in the top 50 firms over the period of 1995–2005.

Sony's Divisions and Financial Sector Analysis by Income

With headquarters located in Minato, Tokyo, Sony now focuses on a wide variety of goods and services such as electronics, gaming and even financial services. As of now, these are split into the following divisions according to the latest Consolidated report: Game & Network Services (G&NS), Music, Pictures, Home Entertainment & Sound (HE&S), Imaging Products & Solutions (IP&S), Mobile Communications (MC), Semiconductors, Financial Services and Other (Sony Corporation, 2019). This kind of specialization into many areas is common for Japanese firms and the idea of vertical integration is very prominent in a lot of major Japanese firms, with Sony being a great example.

Figure 1 demonstrates that the Game & Network Services for Fiscal Year 2018 came in first place in terms of both sales and operating profit with a gain of Yen 133.6 million, thus placing it in front of the Financial Services division, which was barely leading in 2017. However, as can be seen from previous consolidated reports, it was a stable profit generator for Sony for many years.

However, not only is the Game & Network Service (G&NS) division the best performing but it has also become what Sony is known for

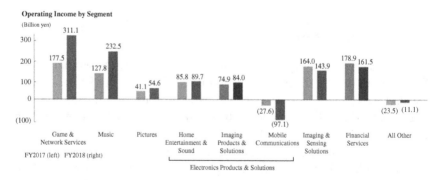

Figure 1.   Overview of Game & Network Service (G&NS) division.

globally, especially by the younger generation. If random people were to be asked what comes into their head when they hear the word Sony, most would say PlayStation. A lot of older folk might refer to electronics since that is what Sony was famous for until the beginning of the 2000s. However, the electronics divisions and especially Mobile Communications have been generating losses over most of the 21st century. And, although electronics is starting to pick up as we can see from FY17 and FY18, mobile phones are still draining Sony's finances.

Sony is also very proud of the G&NS division, describing it as follows in its Corporate Report 2019: "The PlayStation business has created significant value as one of the world's leading entertainment platforms. In addition to establishing a preeminent global position in terms of cumulative units sold, monthly active users, number of titles developed and sales revenue, PlayStation illustrates Sony's approach of "getting closer to people." Getting closer to creators — by providing an environment that makes it easy for developers to do their job. Getting closer to users — by harnessing a variety of data to research user motivations and providing network services that enhance user engagement. The consoles themselves, which link creators and users, incorporate leading-edge technologies that empower creative visions and enable immersive experiences." The report goes on to say that "The PlayStation business has thus become an archetypal Sony business, yet its success is a story that grew from business diversity and has involved overcoming numerous challenges and learning from them" (Sony, 2019a).

This quote from Sony is a very good summary of how and why the PlayStation business is the success it is today. The slogan of "getting closer to people" indicates that Sony has to work closely with all stakeholders ranging from developers of the software to the final consumer. It may sound obvious, but Sony did not always manage to achieve this synergy in the past, which did result in the loss of market share as well as share value, which has quite a positive correlation to Sony's G&NS sector's highs and lows.

History and Analysis of the Game & Network Service Division

The graph in Figure 2 is also from the Sony Corporate Report (Sony, 2019a), and demonstrates the growth of the sector by outlining the profits from its beginning at the end of the 20th Century to the present day. One

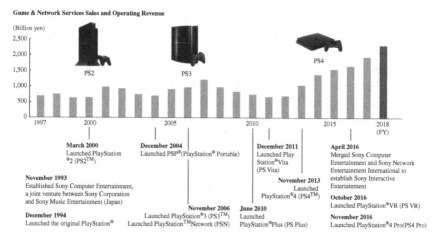

Game & Network Services Sales and Operating Revenue

Figure 2.   PlayStation sales and revenues.

has to keep in mind that although it seems like the division was always growing, its profits were not always as big as they are nowadays. These rough patches will be outlined below.

Establishment of the Division and Its First Product (1993–2000)

Sony did not always have a Game & Network Services division, which only originated out of a failed contract with Nintendo in 1991. At that time, Nintendo had a strong hold on both home and handheld consoles and wanted Sony to develop an add-on for the console which would be able to read compact discs (CDs). However, after reviewing the agreement again around the time Sony was nearly done with the development of the add-on, Nintendo canceled the contract, partnering with Phillips instead due to disagreement over licensing of the software which was to run on the co-developed console. As mentioned in the Sony (2019a), the official statement is as follows: "In 1993 Established Sony Computer Entertainment (renamed Sony Interactive Entertainment in 2016) as a joint venture between Sony Corporation and Sony Music Entertainment (Japan)." The following year, the PlayStation® home video game console was launched in Japan using the technology originally developed for Nintendo. This marked Sony's full-scale entry into the game console business and the establishment of the division.

However, these factors were not always critical parts of G&NS's success. For the first two products, PlayStation 1 and PlayStation 2, there were no or very limited online capabilities present in these two consoles. Therefore, the only thing that mattered was good hardware, which was accommodated with good software for a reasonable price. And, Sony managed to do just that with its first two products.

The launch of the division with the first console was an overwhelming success for Sony, with PlayStation gaining 60%+ of the home console market share, which largely belonged to Nintendo prior to launch. As with all Sony products, its consoles were no exception to being the most high-end pieces of hardware available, especially for entertainment, selling above 100 million units in its lifespan. The innovations in the first PlayStation were also numerous, most noticeably being able to read compact discs, which Sony was to develop for Nintendo but instead kept the technology for itself and capitalized wonderfully on it. However, its success lay not only in the creation of the best piece of entertainment hardware for that time but also in the fact that it managed to appeal to the software developers that breathed life into its creation. The successful relationship between the two parties was giving the consumers the perfect product and carrying Sony way ahead of Nintendo in the home console market segment.

Second Main Product Launch — The PlayStation 2 (2000)

With all the acquired knowledge from its first console launch, Sony released its second console, the PlayStation 2, in the year 2000. This product is a record-holder as of the present day in both the handheld and home console market segments in terms of units sold, estimated at 155 million Yen. This console easily outsold its competitor Microsoft's original Xbox and Nintendo's Game Cube, which both sold just above 20 million units. Although this was mainly due to all the titles being available for the system, which far outnumbered any competitor, there were also other crucial factors at play. First of all, not only was the console capable of playing games but it also doubled as a DVD player. DVD players at the time were as expensive if not more than the newly released PlayStation 2 Console, resulting in people who did not initially plan to play any game buying this console because it could play DVDs, significantly boosting the sales and market domination of this product.

First Handheld Console Release — The PlayStation Portable (2004)

Until December 2004, Sony was only after the home console market segment and left Nintendo to its own devices in the handheld console sector, which gave Nintendo a near monopoly in that sphere. Nintendo reigned supreme in this sector since it launched the Gameboy in 1989, which sold nearly 120 million units in its lifetime, and followed it up with the Gameboy Advanced, which was also hugely successful and sold just above 80 million units (Nintendo, 2019). All this changed with Sony releasing its first portable handheld game, the PlayStation Portable, to compete with Nintendo DS released slightly earlier in 2004. The PSP outperformed Nintendo DS on every single hardware aspect including screen resolution, CPU, memory and storage capabilities as well as connectivity and other multimedia playback, being an overall superior device to the Nintendo DS. Nevertheless, taking all this into account, Nintendo DS still outperformed the PSP by selling a staggering 154.02 million (Nintendo, 2019), making it the highest selling handheld console ever made. PSP on the contrary sold a little under 80 million units as officially stated by Sony (2019b), although other sources point out that it has actually sold a little more than 80 million since the last evaluation. Regardless, not being the best handheld console by sales figures, this was still a big success for Sony since it was its first attempt at the handheld market and it was able to significantly dilute Nintendo's monopoly.

Third Main Product Launch — PlayStation 3 (2006)

Although the previously described step by Sony was significant, Sony's next product release was on a whole other level. If PlayStation 2 was just a very significant hardware update to the PlayStation 1, with some extra features such as DVD playback, the PlayStation 3 was aiming higher than ever with the ambition to "build an immersive game platform capable of connecting to a global network of game consoles" (Sony Corporate Report, 2019). This meant that with this iteration of the mainline product, Sony aimed to make the full use of the Internet and allow the next generation of online play between gamers. Sony planned to achieve this with the launch of PlayStation Network (PSN) which would not only allow players to interact with each other over voice messages, view each other's profiles and most importantly play games together but also get their desired games and other software straight from the PlayStation store instead of having them on discs, as was the case with the other consoles. The work on the PS3 began barely a year after the launch of the PS2, in March 2001, after a partnership between IBM, Toshiba and Sony, and began as a joint venture to develop a cell broadband engine which would become a CPU for the PS3 (Hofstee, 2008). This was incredibly costly for all parties involved and lasted four years. Just to put this power into perspective, "measuring computer performance in FLOPS, the Cell/B.E.'s capacity was 160 times that of PS2 and 40 times that of the latest contemporary personal computers. Some organizations even used PS3s for the creation of Super Computers since it was a lot more money-efficient than the conventional methods" (Buzz, 2006).

Nevertheless, it is worth mentioning that Microsoft released its console (XBOX 360) nearly a year earlier than the PS3 with many of the features already present. And, although not as powerful, it was able to output games at the same quality, and sometimes even better, due to the fact that Sony's ultrapowerful processor had applications outside gaming and was quite a pain for developers who tried to make software on it. At first, Sony was quite arrogant, not even acknowledging Microsoft's console as potential competition, since it was very confident in its new product and still riding on the success of its previous products which were all by far the market leaders in the home console sector. At the start, the new console also cost a staggering $499 for the 20GB variant compared to Xbox 360's $399 price tag. However, even with these high prices, Sony was still making a $300 loss on each console (Staff, 2006), which it was hoping to recover through software sales which were easier than ever to access with the ability to purchase it online at the console.

A lot of challenges followed with the launch of the PS3, and Sony's whole division was riding on its success. If the new PlayStation console was to fail, it could mean shutting down the whole division and leaving a huge dent in the company. And, although in the beginning of the lifecycle, Sony's console was dominated by Microsoft, it managed to recover by significantly cutting the price of the console and pumping out new exclusive software continuously which eventually allowed Sony's console to reach and even overtake the Xbox 360 sales at the end of its lifecycle. It is also important to note that both consoles were outsold by Nintendo's Wii, which sold just above 100 million units in its lifetime (Nintendo, 2019), while both Sony and Microsoft only sold about 85 million units.

Nonetheless, Sony is still very proud of the PS3 and attributes the success of its latest PS4 console to the development and the lessons it learned over the development and lifecycle of the PS3, as can be seen from its corporate report. Moreover, Sony claims that although "initial investment ballooned beyond expectation" (Sony, 2019a), it was of great importance for Sony's other sectors as well as to the success of Sony as a whole. "The hard-earned experience from developing the Cell/B.E. at a massive investment cost led to Sony's semiconductor business capturing the world number one position in imaging application. Applying the advanced MOS LSI technology acquired in developing the Cell/B.E. to the development of CMOS image sensors helped them achieve their superior position. In terms of human resources, system LSI, network and other engineers rapidly cultivated technological skills while Sony brought together hundreds of highly specialized human resources from outside the company. In 2015, for production bases of the semiconductor business, which had undergone restructuring in 2011, Sony announced a program to strengthen development and production of image sensors. Under the third mid-range plan, announced in 2018, Sony intends to maintain its number one position in imaging and becoming the global leader in sensing, both in the CMOS image sensor area. In these ways, the development of the PlayStation business has led to growth that leveraged Sony's business diversity and generated substantial value for other businesses" (Sony, 2019a). This lengthy quote is a demonstration of how the G&NS sector has developed something which was utilized effectively and to great extent in other sectors, making the initial investment well worth it.

Second Handheld Product Release — PlayStation Vita (2011)

There is one product however that Sony has greatly mishandled, which is the successor to its portable handheld PSP. Deep into the lifecycle of the PS3 and two years before the release of the PS4, Sony released a device in December 2011 called the PlayStation Vita (PS Vita) to make a second attempt at the handheld market. Kick-starting the 8th generation of consoles was a handheld from Nintendo named 3DS in late February 2011, incorporating 3D functionality and featuring a double screen like its predecessor. A couple of months later, in December 2011, Sony released its own handheld console in Japan and a couple of months later for the rest of the world. Both consoles were praised for their technology; however, Sony's portable was a step above in every aspect, once again beating Nintendo's handheld in every possible hardware category. Purely from that point of view, it should have easily outsold its competitor; however, in reality, this was not the case. Both consoles were struggling to make projected sales; nevertheless, as years went by, the Nintendo 3DS's sales started to pick up. But, Vita was not selling nearly as well as Sony had hoped. In fact, the sales had become so bad that after 2012, Sony ceased releasing direct sales figures for the Vita in the annual report. In fact, as shown in Figure 3, which demonstrates the sales figures of all the G&NS-related hardware, the sales for the PS Vita are not disclosed. Apart from the date of its release, it is not mentioned in the most recent Sony Corporate Report as well. The reasons for underperformance are vast, including poor pricing strategy, poor marketing, poor support with software, poor relationship with development and failure to acknowledge outside competition such as mobile phones. After a while, it was looking like Sony tried to do everything to wipe the PS Vita from existence as fast as possible by dropping support for it and, recently, altogether admitting it is a legacy device — no longer giving developers a chance to produce games for it on physical cartridges, allowing them to only distribute their games on online platforms.

PlayStation® Hardware	
Cumulative Worldwide Hardware Unit Sales (Sell-in)	
PlayStation®	More than 102.4 million (As of March 31, 2012)
PlayStation®2	More than 155.0 million (As of March 31, 2012)
PSP® (PlayStation®Portable)	More than 76.4 million (As of March 31, 2012)
PlayStation®3	More than 87.4 million (As of March 31, 2017)
PlayStation®4	102.8 million (As of September 30, 2019)

*Sales data on PlayStation®Vita are not disclosed

Figure 3. Strategies and product releases.

Fourth Main Product Launch — PlayStation 4 (2013)

Since the PS Vita was just a side project for Sony, it could brush it aside because its main focus was the home console market and the mainline PlayStation consoles. Instead of supporting it, all resources were shifted to developing and supporting the current console — the PlayStation 4 — which was released in November 2013. In the latest report, Sony says the following on the "Triumphant Return with PlayStation4": "Taking to heart the lessons and challenges taken on with PS3, the development theme for PlayStation 4 was to create a console that would earn the overwhelming support of everyone worldwide." It is clear by this point that Sony has understood from both the rocky lifespan of the PS3 and the commercial failure of the Vita that support of all the parties was needed to create a market leader in the field. "This entailed seeking out what creators and users really want, and reinventing PlayStation as a platform and business with broader appeal — or, in the keywords of the current management policy, getting closer to creators and users" (Sony, 2019a). Sony acknowledges that its previous home console (the PlayStation 3) incorporated many original advanced technologies making it a pain for developers to create software for it. It has adjusted the PlayStation 4 architecture to more closely resemble that of a personal computer, thus making developing for it a whole lot easier. A lot of effort was put in on Sony's side to question and understand what developers truly want from a console, which all added up, and PlayStation once again become the most sold console in the latest generation, easily beating both Microsoft's Xbox One and Nintendo's Switch.

First Virtual Reality (VR) Product Launch — PlayStation VR (2016)

It is also important to acknowledge that SONY is pioneering Virtual Reality hardware as an add-on to its current PlayStation 4, which allows users to play games in virtual reality. Released all the way back in October 2016, it competes very successfully with other big VR brands such as Oculus Rift and HTC Vive. However, if one was to look at the specs, both Oculus and HTC (especially HTC) outperform Sony's VR headset on a hardware level, boasting greater resolution while being able to incorporate the power of a personal computer, which can be significantly more powerful than Sony's console. However, where Sony manages to overtake the other two is the amount of software which is compatible with its VR headset. And, as seen from history, the software tends to be more important than the hardware, which is currently the case as well, since for the three years SONY's VR headset has been released, it has consistently outsold both Facebook's Oculus rift and HTC's VIVE.

Product Sales Summary

The graph below demonstrates all of the consoles Sony has released over the years, as well as their sales figures (Sony, 2019b).

However, it is also important to keep in mind that although the success of the PlayStation hardware is paramount to the overall success of the sector, it is not the only factor that contributes to it. Sony knows this well and outlines the other pieces of the puzzle in its Corporate Report. These can be seen in the illustration below which shows the other key factors which make this division successful. These are PS4 software sold, which are mainly games for the console. However, it also includes movies and music, PSN (Play Station Network) monthly active users (which indicates how frequently people use their console) and PlayStation Plus paid subscribers, which is also a crucial indicator since they pay a monthly/yearly subscription fee to Sony for online features and additional monthly software. The growth of all these factors contributes to the success of this sector (see Figure 4).

At the end of 2020, Sony will release its latest iteration of the home console, the PlayStation 5, which will be a major improvement over its predecessor and is likely to continue the improvement of PSVR, utilizing

Figure 4. PlayStation sales and users 2019 (Sony Interactive Entertainment, 2020).

all the power that the PlayStation 5 will provide. The latest speculations and leaks online also indicate that Sony will continue to pursue VR technology — and, being a market leader in this technology right now, this is a no-brainer. As long as Sony's PlayStation division maintains a close relationship with its suppliers and its consumers, it will continue as the market leader in the segment and will gain a more significant lead in the VR segment as well over its competitors. Furthermore, being proficient in so many other sectors, such as music, film, consumer & professional electronics, as well as financial services, allows Sony to make use of vertical integration. This means that a lot of services can be completed in-house with full transparency, avoiding unnecessary fees and making the process more streamlined. If Sony plays its cards right in the next product release, it can become in the console market what Apple is in mobile market. This means it will not only be producing the console but also the service that comes with it and that is why consumers would want it. The PlayStation Store has already become somewhat similar to the app store on Apple. If Sony can integrate all its products under one umbrella using the same service and being interconnected, it will have no trouble surpassing even Apple. While Apple only focuses on phones and PCs, Sony has a huge range of electronics which can benefit from a combined network while having exclusives such as the PlayStation, which already has a loyal following. All in all, Sony has huge potential where the aforementioned G&NS division has a key role to play in order to realize it.

References

Buzz, I. (2006). Building supercomputer using playstation 3. https://web.archive.org/web/20070206135040/http://www.consolewatcher.com/2006/08/building-supercomputer-using-playstation-3/. (Accessed on January 13, 2020).

Fortune (2020). Sony. Retrieved from Fortune: https://fortune.com/global500/sony/. (Accessed on January 13, 2020).

Hofstee, H. P. (2008). Introduction to the cell broadband engine. Austin: IBM Corporation.

Ingham, T. (2018). Sony is technically the biggest music company in the world (but it's a bit of a stretch) — Music Business Worldwide. Retrieved from Music Business Worldwide: https://www.musicbusinessworldwide.com/sony-technically-biggest-music-company-world-bit-stretch/. (Accessed on February 19, 2020).

Nintendo (2019). Dedicated Video Game Sales Units. Retrieved from nintendo.co.jp: https://www.nintendo.co.jp/ir/en/finance/hard_soft/index.html. (Accessed on December 22, 2020).

Sony (2019a). Corporate Report 2019. https://www.sony.net/SonyInfo/IR/library/corporatereport/CorporateReport2019_E.pdf. (Accessed on November 12, 2020).

Sony (2019b). sie.com. Retrieved from Sony Corporate Data: www.sie.com/en/corporate/data.html. (Accessed on December 12, 2019).

Sony (2020). Sony Japan | 歴史. Retrieved from Sony.co.jp: https://www.sony.co.jp/SonyInfo/CorporateInfo/History/. (Accessed on December 12, 2019).

Sony Corporation (2019). Earnings Announcement. Retrieved from sony.net: https://www.sony.net/SonyInfo/IR/library/presen/er/. (Accessed on December 12, 2019).

Sony Interactive Entertainment 2020. https://www.sie.com/en/corporate/data.html. (Accessed on November 12, 2020).

Staff, E. (2006). iSuppli: 60GB PS3 Costs $840 to Produce. Retrieved from EDGE: https://web.archive.org/web/20111004022638/http://www.next-gen.biz/news/isuppli-60gb-ps3-costs-840-produce. (Accessed on November 16, 2019).

© 2021 World Scientific Publishing Company

https://doi.org/10.1142/9789811231032_0009

Case 9

Reviving a 200-Year-Old Sake Business

Xu Dong and Shiyun Gu

The Failing Sake Company

Sales and consumption of sake — Japan's national drink — have been declining for a long time. Tracing back to 1970s, the sales output of the Japanese national drink began to contract sharply, culminating in a reduction from 1.675 million kiloliters, specifically speaking, to 589,000 kL in 2010, which accounted for one third of the output exclusively 35 years ago (National Tax Agency, 2018). Part of the reason for this condition can be attributed to the diminishing favor of sake among young people, together with the increasing sales of alternatives such as beer, whisky and wine. In the flourishing era, there were more than 3,000 wineries all over the country. However, the number was reduced by half, namely, to around 1,500 in 2014, displaying an overt recession. To some extent, the entire industry is facing a potential reforming promotion. Regardless of those powerful wineries located in the Kansai area, certain local small wineries can only survive with the help of their neighbors.

Yet, much to our surprise, there is still one sake brewery — Asahi Shuzo — trying to subsist in such a decadent situation. Moreover, it is this sake company located in Shutomachi Osogoe, Iwakuni, Yamaguchi Prefecture, the westernmost part of Japan, that produces today's grand DASSAI. Nonetheless, Asahi Shuzo only dealt with ordinary sake called Asahi Fuji — the most popular but very basic sake — at that time. The company had an annual output of 126,000 liters (equivalent to 70,000

113

bottles of 1.8-liter capacity) and sales of 97 million yen for the fiscal year ending in September 1984, which was 85% of the previous year, ranking only No. 4 in Yamaguchi Prefecture. In other words, it was on the verge of bankruptcy. In the same year, Sakurai Hiroshi took over the company from his father at the age of 34.

Asahi Shuzo is not able to compete with other large companies from the perspective of marketing due to its small scale. Sakurai Hiroshi could only figure out trivial promotion activities such as lowering the price, packing the sake in cartons, which makes it prettier, and giving a free gift to buyers of Asahi Shuzo's sake. Sakurai Hiroshi responded to these moves in an interview in Business Weekly: "When I think back on them, they are simply small tricks without being of great avail to long-term performance, contributing to stimulate short-term performance solely" (Wang, 2018). Soon after, a local bar was opened by Asahi Shuzo with an aim to increase sales. Unfortunately, it was visited by just a quarter of the estimated number of customers, leading to a shutdown three months later. After this, not only did the winery make a loss of around half of the revenue at that time but the rumor of the company being on the wane also spread locally.

Confronted with the problem that Asahi Fuji gradually became unsellable in the local market, Sakurai Hiroshi had no choice but to halt production of the ordinary sake Asahi Fuji which has more than a 200-year history.

Surely, this is not the end of story. As the old saying goes, "Confront a person with the danger of death and he will fight to live."

DASSAI — The New Product

Sakurai gained a certain understanding of the market and consumers since he worked as a salesman for almost three years in a big winery in the Kansai area, despite the fact that he knew nothing about brewing. He claimed that Asahi Shuzo had been trying to sell ordinary sake locally, but had not been successful. In trying to figure out why, Sakurai realized that what consumers wanted was high-quality sake with a taste they could truly savor, and he decided that his brewery needed to improve the quality of the sake it produced. As for a target market, youngsters became the very focus. Most young people do not know much about sake; however, they pursue unique and innovative things. Combining both points, the president decided to embark on a new kind of sake (Sakurai, 2018).

That sake was *daiginjo-shu* — a top-quality sake — which was not prevalent in Japan around the 1980s. For most sake breweries, the status of *daiginjo-shu* resembles the top of a pyramid. It is produced in small quantities on the basis of the most demanded table wine and mainly supplied to high-end consumers who pursue quality and a unique way of life.

In the case of *daiginjo-shu* products, extra care needs to be taken. The first step is to start with top-quality rice, easily the best rice for sake brewing. Then, mill away the outer portion, grinding away the outer half or more of each grain before brewing. Usually, more than 40% of each grain of rice needs to be milled, leaving less than 60% of the inner white core, as shown in Figure 1. Using rice processed this way, fermentation is carried out at a low temperature, 5–10 degrees, over a long period of time, more than 30 days (Sato and Kohsaka, 2017).

For Asahi Shuzo, this new venture was its first experience with *ginjo-shu*, and *daiginjo-shu* seemed beyond its wildest dreams. For the rice, Asahi Shuzo used only Yamadanishiki, the top brand of rice suited to brewing sake. Next, as mentioned before, even more of the outer part of the grains was milled away to remove the fat and protein, leaving only the starch behind, leading to the elegant flavor profile that is DASSAI sake. Why is this extravagant? Because this takes advantage of just what is so special about Yamadanishiki. The outer part of proper sake rice is where all the fat and protein reside, with the precious fermentable starches resting safely in the center of the grain. This specially prepared rice is then brewed by young, enthusiastic brewers using clear, clean local water in the isolated, pristine environment of the mountains of Yamaguchi Prefecture, on the southern tip of Honshu, the largest of Japan's four main islands. The result is sake with an identity: delicate, refined and graceful. Naturally, this drives up the price. With *daiginjo-shu*, more often than not, over 50% of the rice grain needs to be milled away which takes 30 hours. Asahi Shuzo had devoted itself to the production process and experienced countless failures in a period spanning about six years, until in 1990, when it successfully developed 50% and 45% sake.

Figure 1. Rice polishing ratio.

The masterpiece, DASSAI 23%, was launched in 1992 and soon came into the picture. Why 23%? Sakurai answered, "We set our goal to the ratio of 25% at first, since 27% is the best known *daiginjo-shu*. Yet, the news that the 24% *daiginjo-shu* is already in the market pushed us to revise the goal to 23%, resulting in another 24 hours required for production." None too soon, Asahi Shuzo commence to produce with a *tôji*, an expert in Sake production. *tôji* master the skills that are forbidden to be inherited beyond their own circle. *tôji* are independent of a brewery, and skills are varied in different cliques. So Sakurai has no idea on how to make sake. Initially, the taste was far from expected and a little bit bizarre, but they, to some extent, improved the production system (Su, 2017). To be more specific, Asahi Shuzo would take charge of the selling, with a *tôji* focusing on brewing. That is how the grand DASSAI 23% was born, becoming a legend and creating a sensation until now (Sakurai, 2014).

New Challenges

The biggest ordeal Sakurai faced was nothing else but the know-how of sake-making. Unfortunately, the two major projects that Sakurai built up painstakingly ended in failure: One was to create a new local beer and the other to operate a self-owned restaurant, resulting in a debt of 190 billion yen (Sakurai, 2018). After that, the sake-makers left the brewery together as the remainder had no experience in making sake. However, the average age of outstanding sake-makers is over 60. Aging is no good and harmful for the company's future development. Consequently, Sakurai decided to take the road of no return — he amassed employees who were young, inexperienced and highly accepting of new things to carry out a new way in factory brewing (Hamaguchi, 2018).

AI Brewing Technology

In the small village of Iwakuni County, Yamaguchi Prefecture, there is a 59-meter steel reinforced concrete building, which is somewhat out of place among the surrounding farmhouses. Surprisingly, it turned out to be a factory for producing sake, which is completely dissimilar to the traditional Japanese-style sake factory in Japan. The new Asahi Brewery, masterminded by Sakurai, pushed the factory into modern industrialization. Producing sake is extremely complicated and some of the crucial steps are as follows: processing material (*seima*); brewing sake (*seikiku*); fermentation (*hakko*); and pressing (*jososhibori*) (Sato and Kohsaka, 2017). First, the factory should be at a constant temperature. Sake has a high-temperature requirement; if there is a slight change within 1–2 degrees, the flavor will be significantly different. A warm and stable environment enables workers to make sake all year round. Second, as per the equipment described on Asahi Shuzo's homepage, the pressing of sake not only utilizes an automatic press for the *moromi* (consisting of steamed rice, *koji*, water and yeast) by pressing air in the tank but also originally introduces a centrifuge to purify *moromi* specially used in DASSAI 23 (official website of Asahi Shuzo, 2018). Third, based on the information released by Fujitsu, which are the providers of the whole technology system, Asahi Shuzo makes a bold trial of AI technology to precisely measure and record the rate of moisture absorption during washing rice, change in moisture in the course of koji making, temperature during preparation, glucose content, amino acidity and change in the proportion of liquor. The technology ensures that different batches of sake are of the same high quality. In addition, Yamadanishiki, a very high-ranking sake rice, is monitored by a cloud system at its plant in Yamaguchi Prefecture. The work will be recorded every day, including the amount of pesticide and fertilizer used, the rice-growing situation, the yield at harvest and quality (Fujitsu, 2018).

By brewing sake in standard operating procedures, Sakurai not only effectively alleviates the shortage of workers but also maintains the stable quality of DASSAI.

Exploring New Markets

Developing the domestic market

When it comes to the graph of changes in volumes of sake consumption and Asahi Shuzo shipments, as shown in Figure 2, it is not hard to see that Asahi Shuzo experienced an astonishing development. The key of Asahi Shuzo's flowering lies in the successful entry into the Tokyo market.

Its first attempt was around the 1990s, coinciding with the collapse of the bubble economy. Later, the aftermath of the collapse could be noticed in Ginza since 1995 as the bars and clubhouses that had been closed were

Figure 2.   Changes in volumes of sake consumption and Asahi Shuzo shipments.

Source: Consumption volume od sake — National Tax Agency Annual Statistics Report (April–March): Shipment volume of Asahi Shuzo — The Beverage & Food Statistics Monthly (January–December).

transformed into Izakaya — Japanese traditional bars. Such a phenomenon opened a window for Asahi Shuzo, since the newborn Izakayas were in dire need of alcohol that was more valuable and upscale. From that time on, DASSAI began to emerge in Tokyo. Notwithstanding, the following growth was not smooth. With the intention to raise awareness of its product, Sakurai opted to visit restaurants and taverns to promote DASSAI from house to house in person, hoping some of them would place DASSAI in the most overt part in the counter area. However, at that time, there was an unwritten rule in the sake industry which said locally produced sake can only be sold locally. People were not optimistic about the Yamaguchi Prefecture-born sake and even doubted whether great sake can be produced in the area to the west of Hiroshima. It is to be noted that compared with breweries in Hiroshima, those in Yamaguchi prefecture are much smaller. In general, Asahi Shuzo's Tokyo expansion was not prosperous so far.

Things did not get better until the firm began to handle the brand issue, for a well-known brand plays a pivotal role in marketing. Among all the promotion activities, it is hard to overstate the significance of the animation Neon Genesis Evangelion, which exerted a profound impact on the youngsters. The director of this animation, Hideaki Anno, made DASSAI the most favorable drink of one of the characters, Katsuragi Misato, and took a close-up. Evangelion has developed into a social phenomenon beyond its primary fan base, generating national discussion in Japan

(Wikipedia, 2020). Moreover, not only did the animation prefer DASSAI but also Japanese enterprises had a partiality for it. It is common to find DASSAI at the opening ceremonies of Uniqlo's new stores, whether in Ginza, Paris, Bangkok or New York. DASSAI had already become part of the corporate culture, but with Prime Minister Abe Shinzo being the "salesman" and Obama and Putin being the "spokespersons", Asahi Shuzo finally found its own niche. On October 7, 2013, the Japan–Russia summit was held during APEC (Asia-Pacific Economic Cooperation), and this coincided with Putin's 61st birthday. Needless to say, Abe Shinzo sent Putin a bottle of DASSAI to celebrate his birthday. On April 23, 2014, Abe also invited President Barack Obama to enjoy DASSAI when he visited Japan. Obama was exceedingly fond of it and returned home with one as a souvenir. This series of diplomatic activities was soon caught by mass media and became known to the broader population. To crown it all, Prime Minister Abe, Tadashi Yanai of Uniqlo and director Hideaki Anno are all from Yamaguchi Prefecture, the birthplace of Asahi Shuzo. We can tell that Asahi Shuzo entered the Tokyo market successfully somewhat by luck and also by considerable contribution from compatriots.

Developing the Export Market

With competition in Tokyo becoming ever fiercer, the company's top priority was to develop an international market for its product. "One of the things that makes us unique is that we have not targeted existing sake drinkers. This helped us to avoid getting tangled up in competition within the industry in Japan. From now on, our only choice is to develop our market outside Japan," Sakurai said, comparing his situation to that of French wine makers who have developed expensive lines for overseas markets.

Asahi Shuzo's first overseas venture was in 2002, when the company's products went on sale in Taiwan. Distribution to the United States came the following year. The recent popularity of Japanese cuisine has seen increasing numbers of fashionable Japanese restaurants opening in New York. "People are reluctant to spend a lot of money on something they have not tried before. So, the best way to win new customers is to introduce them to sake in restaurants. Recently, wine shops are starting to stock Asahi Shuzo sake too."

Asahi Shuzo's sake is now available in 18 countries worldwide, including Dubai, Hong Kong, Britain and France (Official Website of Asahi Shuzo, 2018). Sales outside Japan account for approximately 10%

of the brewery's turnover and the most important market after the United States is France. "France has a very strong influence on the States as far as food is concerned. If we can't sell well in France, it will be difficult to sell in the States too," said Sakurai.

This was the reason Asahi Shuzo brewery decided to take the bold step of opening an exclusive outlet in France. On March 23, 2014, the brewery's first overseas shop opened in Paris. The outlet was modeled on the Dassai Bar 23 that opened in May, 2013, in Kyobashi, Tokyo. This is a directly managed store that combines a bar and a shop. "Unless we can sell globally, there is no future for sake." In line with this principle, Asahi Shuzo brewery is aiming to increase overseas sales to 50% of total sales.

According to statistics on exports from the National Tax Agency, the export volume of sake for 2012 was 14,131 kL (¥8.946 billion). Exports have reached a new record for three years running. With traditional Japanese cuisine designated as an Intangible Cultural Heritage by UNESCO in 2013, the popularity of Japanese food and drink seems set to go from strength to strength (see Figure 3).

No longer will it be a small sake brewery tucked away in the mountains of Yamaguchi. Asahi Shuzo brewery will be reborn as a major player in the fast-developing global market for high-quality Japanese sake.

The Future

DASSAI positioned itself in the domestic sake market as a young person's favorite with its smooth taste and fruity smell, concreting its position.

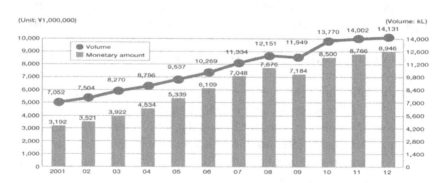

Figure 3. Trends in exports of sake. (National Tax Agency, 2018).

Source: National Tax Agency export Statistics (January–December).

DASSAI has many competitors in sake categories, but the most powerful competition is Japanese beer. When young people come to the Izakaya, they first order a glass of beer or a cocktail (ZUU). This is a dietary habit which is hard to change across all major cities. In order to cater to young people, many sake-makers have launched sparkling sake with a cheaper price and lovely packaging style. The strategy adopted by these sake-makers is to add new product lines. Asahi Shuzo actually has released the DASSAI 39 and DASSAI 50 sparkling versions recently. It seems like Asahi Shuzo considers a similar strategy to increase its market share. But, time is needed to see if it works or not.

Sakurai not only makes a bucket of money in the domestic market but he is also ambitious and hopes DASSAI will become a status symbol of overseas celebrities. In France, for example, due to high tariffs and other taxes, the price of DASSAI has been doubled. If it appears in an upmarket restaurant, the retail price will be higher. Costly gourmet food and drinks are only for the rich who can afford it. Sakurai has locked the customer base — the high-income group — but it is a long way from branding abroad. Wines and champagnes have been in the upscale market for a very long time. There are considerable complex issues about how to build DASSAI to be a luxury brand, which distribution channels to be utilized and how to modify sake to adapt to the local food culture.

The surging demand in both the domestic and international markets has brought unprecedented opportunities to Sakurai, but the balance between productive capacity and quality is hard to find. The reason is that the process of making sake is so sophisticated that you still need a large number of craftsmen to operate, especially in the stage of sake brewing and material processing. Choosing high-volume production is likely to result in lower quality (Kouji, 2017).

On the contrary, material shortage affected many breweries. This was due to the material — Yamadanishiki. There is only one material that is Yamadanishiki; however, Yamadanishiki is a kind of premium sake-making rice, and the price is 1.5 times higher than the ordinary sake-making rice. Still, it did little to dampen the enthusiasm of the breweries, and above all, one-tenth of all Yamadanishiki of Japan is supplied to Asahi Shuzo. Asahi Shuzo has invested in modern technology equipment for the farmers, so the production capacity has been greatly expanded. Nonetheless, considering that other breweries also need Yamadanishiki, the materials that can be obtained are still limited (Sato, 2014).

Obviously, Sakurai will not choose to lower the quality and destroy his own hard-built brand, which he takes pride in for laying the foundation of the whole company. However, the status quo is that shipments are not relatively stable and market penetration is unlikely to rise. It has been a long trajectory, but Asahi Shuzo has the signature product. The future of Asahi Shuzo looks promising.

Questions

1. What are the competitive advantages of Asahi Shuzo?
2. Asahi Shuzo was a very small brewery ranked 4th in Yamaguchi. What kind of reform did Asahi Shuzo do?
3. What actions should Asahi Shuzo take to balance the relation between capacity and quality?
4. Still, DASSAI is far from the most famous sake in Japan, but it was loved by people outside Japan and treated as the representation of sake. What strategies should Asahi Shuzo develop next to survive in the international market?

References

Fujitsu. (2018). http://pr.fujitsu.com/jp/news/2018/04/19.html. (Accessed on April 19, 2018).

Hamaguchi, S. (2018). ピンチをチャンスに変えてきた——旭酒造・桜井会長が振り返る「獺祭」と歩んだ日々". *ITMEDIA*. https://www.itmedia.co.jp/business/articles/1809/13/news056.html. (Accessed on September 13, 2018).

Hamaguchi, Shotaro. *pinchi o chansu ni kaete kita — Asahi shuzō Sakurai kaichō ga furikaeru 'dassai' to ayunda hibi*. ITMEDIA. Web. 13. September 2018 <http://www.itmedia.co.jp>.

Kouji, A. (2017). Study on internationalization of Japanese manufacturing SME's: A case study of Asahi Shuzo Co., Ltd. 'DASSAI'. *Journal of the Faculty of Management and Information Systems, Prefectural University of Hiroshima*, 10, p. 47–56.

National Tax Agency. (2018). National Tax Agency Annual Statistics Report". National Tax Agency. *http://www.nta.go.jp/english/publication/agency_report/index.htm*. (Accessed on November 17, 2018).

Official Website of Asahi Shuzo (2018). Distributors list. *http://www.asahishuzo.ne.jp/en/*. (Accessed on November 21, 2018).

Sakurai, H.(2018). *rìběn dì yī míngjiǔ de chóngshēng xiāoshòu zhī*. Kadokawa Taiwan.

Sakurai. H. (2014). *gyakkyō keiei — yamaoku no jizake ʼdassaiʼ o sekai ni todokeru gyakuten hassō-hō*. Diamondo, Tokyo.

Sato, J. and Kohsaka, R. (2017). Japanese sake and evolution of technology: A comparative view with wine and its implications for regional branding and tourism. *Journal of Ethnic Foods,* 4. pp. 88–93.

Sato, J. (2014). *kome ga tarinai*. Tsuka Economic Monthly Report 6, pp. 6–7.

Su, H. (2017). Rìběn shānkǒu xiàn: Jiàngrén jiàngxīn chū jīngpǐn. http://m.fx361. com/news/2017/0313/1104880.html. Accessed November 12, 2020.

Wang, Z. (2018). *shùjù niàng de rìběn guóyàn jiǔ 70 nián tǎ jì zhuǎnxíng chóngshēng jì*. Business Weekly, 20 June 2018. https://www.businessweekly. com.tw/magazine/Article. Accessed November 12, 2020.

Wikipedia (2020). *https://en.wikipedia.org/wiki/Neon_Genesis_Evangelion# Production.* (Accessed November 12, 2020).

ZUU online.com (2017). tāgetto wa kokunai nomi narazu ʼdassaiʼ no sekai shin-shutsu senryaku no genjitsumi. https://zuuonline.com/archives/177392. Accessed November 12, 2020.

Corporate Growth

© 2021 World Scientific Publishing Company
https://doi.org/10.1142/9789811231032_0010

Case 10

TOTO's Washlet Going International

Martha Denis

TOTO has been manufacturing bathroom ceramics for almost a century and is the undisputable market leader in Japan. The company introduced its star product, the Washlet, back in 1980 and its success made TOTO a household name in the industry.

Currently, it is estimated that over 36 million Washlets have been sold worldwide; however, in the beginning, TOTO struggled domestically and the first launch of the Washlet was a failure. The company was quick to adapt after listening to customer complaints and hesitations about the product. In order to grow the domestic market, the company relied on strategic partnerships, technology innovation and marketing strategies to generate interest in their products. With the aging population and reduced construction projects, TOTO's domestic focus has been on the remodeling industry and R&D development of green technologies for bathrooms and other applications.

Internationally, the company has steadily gained a market share in the Americas, China, Asia and Europe and each country has required the implementation of different management strategies. Most importantly, the focus will be on the steps TOTO has taken to achieve its long-term management plan that, among other things, sets specific sales targets for each region. In understanding how TOTO operates domestically and inter-nationally, theoretical considerations about the Confucian influence in Japan, the effectiveness of Japanese management practices and the strate-gic thinking of managers must be taken into account.

TOTO — A Traditional Japanese Company

The presence of Confucianism in Japan can be dated back to the 6th or 7th century, with concepts of loyalty, self-discipline, gratitude and the role of leaders, subordinates and the self-development since that time; "the preferred leadership style" of a Confucian society like Japan stresses the importance of "the search for perfection and the development of a righteous character" (Dollinger, 1988).

Three main factors underlie Japanese management processes — a long-run planning horizon, commitment to lifetime employment and collective responsibility — as potential causes behind certain management practices that include, to name a few, discipline and order in work, reduced turnover and high loyalty and trust and interdependence.

Kenichi Ohmae (1982) provides insight into the strategic mind of Japanese managers in organizations looking to maximize profits, resolve conflict and overcome obstacles across industries. Ohmae, a Japanese organizational theorist and management consultant, offers a multitude of paradigms with comprehensive solutions to problems corporations might face internally and externally.

Company background

"Kindness must always come first. Bring the concept of service to your work. Your goal should be to provide good products and satisfy the customer. Accomplish that, and profit and compensation will follow. Many in this world chase after the shadow of profit. But, in the end, they never capture the real thing." — Kazuchika Okura, Founder (TOTO Corporate Report, 2016, p. 1).

TOTO's foundation dates back to May 15, 1917, and its headquarters can still be found in Kitakyushu, Fukuoka. In 1912, Kazuchika Okura began developing sanitary ceramics and by 1914, he produced Japan's first seated ceramic flush toilet. Three years later, he founded Toyo Toki Co. Ltd., Oriental Ceramics Company, its meaning in Japanese, in the port town of Kokura, Kitakyushu, which focused on the production of sanitary ware. The Great Kanto earthquake of 1923 heavily damaged the existing waste management systems in the Kanto and Tohoku regions resulting in the reconstruction of this system.

With a new sewerage system in place, the company saw a boost in demand for its products, which continued until World War II. After the war ended, the company expanded into production of bathroom faucets and fittings using metal, and by 1964, Toyo Toki Co. Ltd. produced the first prefabricated bathroom module, just in time for the Tokyo Olympics. At the time, Japan was enjoying a period known as the "economic miracle" — a time of rapid economic growth characterized by a boom in the construction industry. This industrialization policy introduced by Prime Minister Hayato Ikeda, and executed with support from Japan's Ministry of International Trade and Industry (MITI), laid the foundation for construction companies in terms of their ability to build the infrastructure needed to host an internationally renowned event.

As for Okura's company, this meant mass installations of his prefabricated bathroom modules in hotels and other public places. In 1970, Toyo Toki Co. Ltd. was shortened to TOTO, and in 1980, with the launch of the Washlet, TOTO became a recognized brand associated with cleanliness, comfort and lifestyle.

The Washlet — TOTO's Besteller

The Washlet, a TOTO trademark, is undeniably the company's most popular and bestselling product with sales of over 36 million units worldwide. The Washlet is an electronic bidet with a water spraying system for personal cleaning. It has evolved over the years since it was first introduced into the Japanese market in 1980, going from an electric toilet cover to an integrated bidet system. Some key features worth mentioning include the following: the heated toilet seat that warms up to body temperature, the operation panel that allows users to control functions and save their settings, the deodorizer that hides any unpleasant smells, the antibacterial wand that sprays cleansing water and, lastly, the warm air dryer conveniently located under the toilet seat.

The beginnings of the Washlet can be traced back to the American Sitzbath, an invention of Arnold Cohen, founder of the American Bidet Company. In the early 1960s, Cohen's father had a serious medical condition that made it difficult for him to comfortably use the toilet. As a result, Cohen conceived the first idea of a toilet with an integrated bidet system and aimed to distribute it to hospitals to be used by patients with difficulty around using the toilet and cleaning themselves. His first design included two features that are still present in the Washlet, the warm-water-spraying nozzle and a dryer that blew hot air into the user's intimate parts. Enthusiasm for the American Bidet Company and their revolutionary

American Sitzbath fell short as the company failed to break cultural taboos around their product and many advertisers refused to run their ads. After the letdown, Cohen licensed his invention and patent to TOTO and the Japanese company launched a rebranded version in Japan called the Wash Air Seat with no success.

By 1980, TOTO developed its own version of the toilet bidet system known as a Washlet. The first TOTO model to be introduced into the Japanese market was the Washlet G, which introduced, apart from the original features found in the Sitzbath, a heated toilet seat (Figure 1).

TOTO made a point of installing Washlets in public spaces, restaurants, hotels, airports and even on a JAL Boeing 787 (Japan Airlines Press Releases, 2015) as a strategy to give their product more exposure. From 1987 onwards, the Washlet evolved dramatically and TOTO launched several models, which include the following: the integrated Washlet (1987), Neorest (1993), travel Washlet (1995) and Actilight (2013). Similarly, the technology associated with the Washlet also developed tremendously and the latest product launch features a one-of-a-kind photocatalytic technology that utilizes UV light that keeps the Washlet clean by

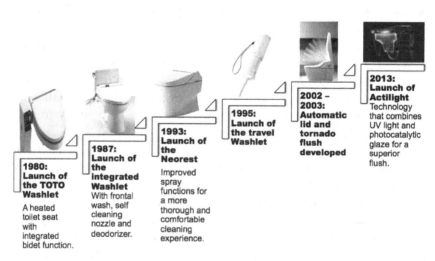

Figure 1. The history of the Washlet and Washlet sales worldwide (www.toto.com, 2020).

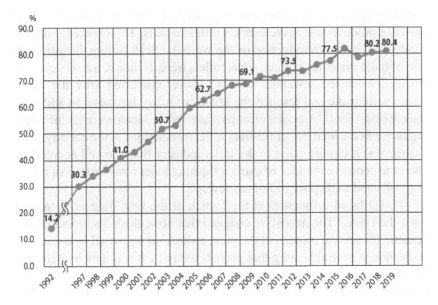

Figure 2. The proliferation of spray seats in Japan (Japan Sanitary Industry Association, 2020).

making it difficult for dirt to attach to the bowl, and for an environmentally friendly flush.

Steadily, Washlet sales grew and the company reached market saturation in Japan at 70% of the market share (Nogata, 2014). According to data from the Japanese Cabinet Office, bidets in a two-or-more-person household have increased in Japan over the years and by 2019, adoption rate was at 80.4%, having started at 14.2% in 1992 (Japan Sanitary Equipment Industry Association, 2020) (Figure 2).

Success strategies

Success did not come easily for TOTO. The introduction of the first Washlet in 1967 was a complete failure, due to two main reasons: the product was too expensive for the market, and the customers were not convinced of the value proposition of the product. Parallels can be drawn between the struggles TOTO and Joseph Gayetty faced when promoting their products. The latter has been attributed with the mass commercialization of toilet paper, after overcoming societal taboos around a product used to clean one's intimate parts. TOTO faced a similar challenge with the introduction of the Wash Air Seat. Before the introduction of bidet systems to Japan, squat toilets were the norm, but this quickly changed when the sewerage system was reconstructed after the Great Kanto earthquake and reached the homes of many Japanese. In addition, after World War II, American troops stationed in Japan were an influencing factor in the increase of flushing toilet installations in the country. This change was a turning point in the toilet industry that allowed people like Okura to conceive the idea of using a flushing toilet bowl instead of a hole in the ground to dispose of human sewage.

TOTO faced difficulties at the launch of the first Washlet, imported from the USA. "The new style changed that now: flesh, had to sit on icy ceramic for several months of the year, a situation worsened by a national resistance to central heating that persists today … It was a niche item that TOTO thought had mass appeal. But their version failed. It was too expensive. The bidet function was too foreign" (George, 2008a, p. 36). TOTO was quick to identify an opportunity for improvement and introduced a heating function for the toilet seat. However, getting the public to embrace the Washlet required more than an added feature again. "But in the 1970s, when Toto turned to relaunching the Washlet, the toilet, — bidet or otherwise — had no place in conversation. It was something detached, unmentionable, out of sight and smell. It could not be advertised" (George, 2008a, p. 37).

Consequently, TOTO focused on implementing three key elements in order to penetrate the local market. First, it developed strategic partnerships with wholesalers, for their channels of distribution, and construction companies, for their support with design modifications to facilitate installations in housing complexes. An obstacle that TOTO had to overcome was getting construction companies and architects to redesign bathrooms in such a way that power plugs were easily accessible for the toilet because Washlets need electricity to work. After the Japanese asset price bubble crash of 1992, the repercussions of the downfall of the construction industry were strongly felt by TOTO. Without the ability to sell to the construction market, the company turned to the remodeling industry and partnered with plumbers and contractors on an initiative called the "remodel club". The arrangement connected potential buyers at showrooms with members of the club that were TOTO trained and approved.

Even though 1999 to 2003 overlapped with Japan's Lost Decade, a time period characterized by slow and stagnant economic growth, sales of bathroom products still increased by 250% (Tilin and Mikami, 2004).

The second contributing factor to the growth of the company was the rapid rate of adoption of the Washlet. The public, having been exposed to the Washlet since the 1960s, was familiar with the product and this reduced resistance or rejection of new product launches. Familiarity with the product is crucial to sell a Washlet, as mentioned by President Madoka Kitamura in an interview (The Worldfolio, 2015): "With the Washlet, people do not tend to think in terms of high-tech or low-tech. If they have never used it, they will not understand how it will feel or improve their lives." The message being conveyed was that only through personally experiencing the novelty of the Washlet could a potential consumer determine their willingness to purchase the product.

The third factor that contributed to the success of TOTO in Japan was their marketing strategy. TOTO first launched the Washlet in the 1980s, but the product had little success in the market due to its perceived high price by consumers and a lack of education regarding its value and use. However, by 1985, TOTO had sold a million units of the Washlet and sales continued to rise. Unlike TOTO, its main competitor, another Japanese company called Inax, was unsuccessful despite having first-mover advantage. Inax had introduced a toilet with bidet function long before TOTO; it was called Shower Toilet because of the cleaning function of the retractable wand (Figure 3).

Figure 3. Screenshots of (left) TOTO and Inax washlet commercials in the 1980s (Tooaleta Dusch WC Zentrum (2014) and gazoboxoldcm (2007)).

Success can also be credited to TOTO's memorable advertisements. One in particular, from 1982, featured singer Jun Togawa next to a TOTO Washlet. By the end of the commercial, she turned her back to the viewer and the phrase "おしりだって　洗ってほしい" which roughly translates to "bottoms want to be cleaned too" appeared on the screen. It was appealing and unforgettable for consumers. In stark contrast was the commercial by Inax, featuring a gorilla clumsily trying to figure out how to use the cleaning function while sitting on the toilet bowl (George, 2008b).

Technological innovation

TOTO has pioneered innovation of sanitary ware technology since the 1980s and enjoyed considerable success manufacturing products with an array of consumer applications. The latest figures indicate sales of the TOTO Washlet have surpassed 50 million units sold worldwide (PR Newswire Association, 2019), making TOTO a household name in the industry. Clearly, TOTO's core competency is R&D, and usages of their technology range from Washlets to tiles and the semiconductor industry (TOTO Corporate Report, 2016).

Behind the technological innovation at TOTO is the company's commitment to and investment in a clear mission, vision and long-term management plan. With over a century since the company's establishment, TOTO has been successful in articulating the value proposition to customers as well as continuously improving the functionality of their products. At the forefront of the technological developments at TOTO is the Washlet with its unique features: the twin tornado cleansing system, CeFiONtect dirt-resistant toilet bowl glazing and ewater+ functionality that sprays the toilet bowl with antibacterial electrolyzed water to keep it clean for longer (TOTO Corporate Report, 2016). Furthermore, Hokkarari floors with double-layered thermal insulation, Air-in-Shower technology that is water efficient and the insulated thermal pot "Mahobin" bathtub that maintains the temperature of baths for longer are all part of the core products and technology at TOTO (TOTO Corporate Report, 2015). President Kitamura details the intricacies in the manufacturing of the ceramics. "Our toilets are very complex. They require an intricate structure to generate a centrifugal cyclonic action of the water spinning around the rim. It looks like a simple action, but it requires a particular type of gas kiln to fire this kind of ceramics" (The Worldfolio, 2015).

Aside from the company's unique technologies developed through R&D, for 2019, the company focused on cross-organizational innovation activities, consisting of marketing innovation, management resource innovation and demand chain innovation (TOTO Group Integrated Report, 2019). The aim of each activity is to highlight different aspects of the products and the company. The emphasis for marketing innovation is promotion of key design, functionality and initiatives of company and products. For management resource innovation, the goal is to attract the best talent to the company by creating an inclusive and flexible environment. Lastly, the challenge with demand chain innovation is reorganizing supply chain structures and promoting manufacturing worldwide (TOTO Group Integrated Report, 2019).

Global Expansion

TOTO's global success is unmatched by its competitors and the company's network continues to expand. Overseas business accounts for 22% of consolidated net sales for FY2018 compared to 8% in FY2001 (TOTO Group Integrated Report, 2019). The company positioned itself strategically in the international market and approached foreign customers in three main stages: brand awareness creation, key partnerships for market penetration and strengthening of network contacts to establish TOTO as a luxury brand. Through the installation of products in popular and public locations like hotels and airports, the launch of TOTO showrooms and the development of seminars and presentations, TOTO was able to break into the international scene and make its mark. The company has presence in 18 countries with 14 showrooms globally and the forecast for FY2019 is expected to show an increase in net sales in Asia, the Americas and Europe (TOTO Group Integrated Report, 2019).

Madoka Kitamura has been serving as President and Representative Director since April 2014, having joined TOTO in 1981. The company's global workforce consists of 35,431 employees and TOTO is present in 16 countries. Subsidiaries, affiliates, factories, showrooms and sales offices can be found across the world, in places like the USA, Mexico, Brazil, China, Singapore, UAE, Philippines, Thailand, Vietnam, Malaysia, India, Indonesia, Taiwan, Korea, Germany, United Kingdom and France. Additionally, for sales purposes, the company has divided itself into three regions, Japan, China & Asia, and Americas & Europe, and each contributes to TOTO's core businesses.

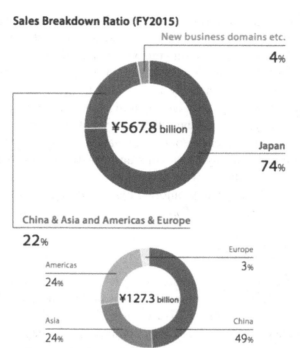

Figure 4.   TOTO global sales breakdown FY2015 (TOTO Corporate Report, 2016).

According to the TOTO Corporate Report for 2016, the company's core businesses are the domestic housing equipment business, overseas housing equipment business and new business domains; similarly, the report provides a sales breakdown of global sales. For the 2015 fiscal year (ending March 31), the company had net sales of ¥567.8 billion of which Japan contributed 74% (¥420.3 billion). China & Asia and Americas & Europe made up 22% (¥127.3 billion) of global sales with the following dissection: China 49%, America 24%, Asia 24% and Europe 3%. Finally, new business domains made up 4% of global sales (¥19.8 billion) (Figure 4).

TOTO's long-term management plan

TOTO conceived a strategic framework with the goal of becoming a "truly global company by 2017" (TOTO Corporate Report, 2016) and to increase net sales to ¥650 billion by the 2017 fiscal year. The plan to increase sales will be done through the strengthening of corporate governance and innovation. The company has implemented several strategies in order to achieve this goal for each of its core businesses.

In the domestic market, TOTO faces an aging population, which means that in the future, the number of new construction projects will be limited. Therefore, the emphasis is on the remodeling segment that is growing alongside the green remodeling business in partnership with TDY (TOTO, Daiken and YKK AP). The company is also an official partner for the 2020 Tokyo Olympics and Paralympics and will provide plumbing products and services as part of the agreement (The Tokyo Organising Committee of the Olympic and Paralympic Games, 2016) (Figure 5).

For overseas business, the company is focusing on creating new markets and driving the growth of existing and new product lines. In China, the growing middle class and influx of Chinese tourists to Japan present an opportunity for the company to continue to increase its sales. In America, TOTO is targeting luxury and high-end consumers and locations in order to slowly transition into the mainstream market, including the luxury hotel The Kitano in New York (Pfanner and Fukase, 2014). In Europe, TOTO continues to develop channels of distribution for its products and increase product awareness through key partnerships and installations.

TOTO V-Plan 2017 was an initiative by the company's President, Mr. Kitamura. When asked in an interview what he believed was the main challenge faced by the company in achieving the 2017 plan, he expressed, "We want to manufacture products that our customers want. Unlike many companies, however, we do not make products that people replace every

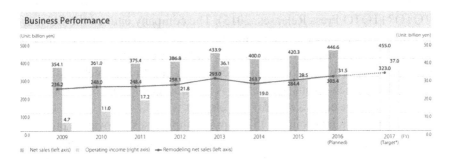

Figure 5.   TOTO projected results and targets (TOTO Corporate Report, 2016).

Notes: This Medium-term Management Plan based on assumptions, estimates and plans as of May 23, 2014.

year" (The Worldfolio, 2015). The European market presents an interesting challenge when it comes to achieving the goals set in the 2017 plan. TOTO's market share in China or America has only been possible after many decades of steady growth.

In Europe, TOTO is a relatively new player with plans for gradual expansion, as Mr. Kitamura expressed: "We want to be a company whose products are loved by the country where we sell them. That is what we value" (The Worldfolio, 2015). In developing products for the international market, TOTO values technological innovation, and in Europe, this has been particularly important to attract attention for TOTO products. Mr. Kitamura elaborates, "Yes, we innovated the whirlpool technology and brought it to the general public. Through an exhibition that is held every two years in Europe, our products have become known worldwide" (The Worldfolio, 2015).

Residential equipment focuses on the production and distribution of urinals, sinks, washbasins, toilets, Washlets, plumbing accessories and kitchens to name a few; contrarily, new business domain products include high-precision ceramics for semiconductors, plasma displays and fiber optics as well as green building materials with added Hydrotech technology.

The European market presents a challenge

According to an interview with Soichi Abe, Nat TOTO, Europe is one of the most difficult markets to enter: "No other continent has tougher competition or higher standards of quality. There are so many well-established companies in Europe already, and no-one was waiting for a company like TOTO" (TOTO Press Releases, 2015). The company entered the EU market in 2009 and sales in the region for the 2015 fiscal year were at 3%. The strategic focus, according to Abe, has been on differentiation. In the case of Europe, the emphasis has been on quality through technology and not design, which means that design is an important aspect of the product, but it is showcased in a tasteful and elegant way.

TOTO participates in the ISH fair and showcases innovative products to the European market. The introduction of the rimless toilet integrated with CeFiONtect glaze and tornado flush technology was a calculated move for the European market, and an important selling point for the company has been its use of green technologies. TOTO products are aligned with the company's philosophy of conserving and caring for the environment, so they are resource saving in terms of water consumption. The technology that goes into the design of the material for the Washlet makes it difficult for dirt to attach to the bowl, keeping the Washlet clean and saving on water and cleaning products (The Worldfolio, 2015).

Furthermore, in Europe, TOTO has also fostered strategic partnerships with luxury hotels like the ShangriLa, Hilton, Mandarin Oriental and Ritz Carlton to name a few. These alliances have worked because customers staying at five-star hotels expect luxury and TOTO products are in line with this expectation (TOTO Press Release, 2015). The company has also partnered with European manufacturing and design businesses; in 2013, at ISH, TOTO announced its collaboration with German ceramics manufacturer Villeroy & Boch AG (TOTO Press Releases, 2013). TOTO has also worked with designer Stefano Giovannoni and the Elium Design agency to develop unique products for the European market.

In the long run, the company is looking to introduce its star product, the Washlet, alongside other bathroom products. However, company efforts are concentrated on the remodeling business, which brings in higher revenue margins, and public spaces, which is where the product gets exposure to mainstream customers. By the 2017 fiscal year, TOTO expected sales in Europe to increase, in combination with sales in China, Asia and America, from ¥127.3 billion to ¥158 billion, in accordance with the TOTO V-Plan 2017.

Conclusion

When examining the position of TOTO in different markets, there is a significant contrast in terms of success. The company has adapted its go-to-market strategies to meet the needs and requirements of different markets. From a theoretical perspective, the research on Japanese management by Marc J. Dollinger (1988), J. Bernard Keys and Tomas R. Miller (1984), and Kenichi Ohmae (1982) is present in TOTO's management practices and provides insight into the values and principles underlying Japanese business and management practices.

According to the company philosophy, TOTO strives to create products that benefit and bring happiness to humans and the environment alike. Moreover, the TOTO V-Plan 2017 is a long-term management goal that sets the tone for actions the company must undertake in the coming years to be able to achieve this goal. In this regard, a long-term planning horizon and collective accountability — concepts researched by Keys and Miller (1984) — are considered key factors in the success of the Japanese management approach.

Almost a century after its foundation, TOTO's leadership position is unmatched in the local market, but this is not the case overseas. TOTO's strategies in America, Asia, China and Europe have varied significantly and evolved with their products. In America and China, TOTO is experiencing growth and expansion, but sales in Europe are not at the same level. Will TOTO catch up to its competitors in the European market?

Questions

1. How has the company adapted its strategies in different markets?
2. Will TOTO be able to emulate its domestic success in Europe?
3. What can TOTO teach us about barriers to entry to new markets?
4. What are TOTO's core competencies?

References

Dollinger, M.J. (1988). Confucian Ethics and Japanese Management Practices. *Journal of Business Ethics*, 7, pp. 575–584.

gazoboxoldcm. (2007). *198X INAX* シャワートイレ [Video File]. https://www.youtube.com/watch?v=UaOdP1D_B30. (Accessed on January 25, 2017).

George, R. (2008a). The Robo-Toilet Revolution. In *The big necessity: The unmentionable world of human waste and why it matters* (pp. 33–48).

George, R. (2008b). *Japan's hi-tech toilets*, The Telegraph. from http://www.telegraph.co.uk/technology/3358291/Japans-hi-tech-toilets.html. (Accessed on January 25, 2017).

Japan Sanitary Industry Association (2020). https://www.sanitary-net.com/global/about/.

Japan Airlines Press Releases (2015). *JAL SKY SUITE 787 Service To Include New Boing 787-9 International Service ~ JAL sky suites 787 offers more space to customers in JAL economy class ~.*, from http://press.jal.co.jp/en/release/201501/003723.html. (Accessed on January 25, 2017).

Keys, J.B. and Miller, T.R. (1984). *The Japanese Management Theory Jungle*. *The Academy of Management Review*, 9(2), pp. 342–353.

Nogata, D.J. (2014). *Do You Washlet? TOTO's Challenge in Breaking into Mainstream America*. https://docplayer.net/31726853-Do-you-washlet-toto-s-challenge-in-breaking-into-mainstream-america-dj-nogata-president-ceo-toto-americas-holdings-inc-apr.html. (Accessed on January 25, 2017).

Ohmae, K. (1982). *The mind of the strategist: The art of Japanese business*. New York: McGraw-Hill.

Pfanner, E. and Fukase, A. (2014). *Smart Toilets Arrive in US, Japanese Commode Manufacturers Target New Market*, The Wall Street Journal. http://www.wsj.com/articles/smart-toilets-arrive-in-u-s-1401160563. (Accessed on 25 January 25, 2017).

PR Newswire Association (2019). *Global Sales of TOTO's Popular WASHLET® Line exceed 50 Million*. from https://www.prnewswire.com/news-releases/global-sales-of-totos-popular-washlet-line-exceed-50-million-300942706.html. (Accessed on December 25, 2019).

The Tokyo Organising Committee of the Olympic and Paralympic Games (2020). Tokyo 2020 Welcomes TOTO as an Official Partner. https://tokyo2020.org/en/news/sponsor/20160224-02.html. (Accessed on December 25, 2019).

Tilin, A. and Mikami, M. (2004). *Heir to the Throne Flush with success in Japan, TOTO Ltd. next wants to conquer America with its wondrous high-tech toilets*, Business 2.0 Magazine TOTO (2016). *TOTO Corporate Report 2016*. http://www.toto.co.jp/en/company/profile/library/. (Accessed on January 25, 2017). http://money.cnn.com/magazines/business2/business2_archive/2004/08/01/377392/ (Accessed on January 25, 2017).

The Worldfolio (2015). *Toto: Experiencing is believing*. from http://www.theworldfolio.com/interviews/toto-experiencing-is-believing/3663/. (Accessed on January 25, 2017).

Toilet Navigation, Japan Sanitary Equipment Industry Association. https://www.sanitary-net.com/global/about/. (Accessed on December 25, 2017).

Tooaleta Dusch Wc Zentrum. (2014). TOTO Washlet 1982 Reklame [Video File]. from https://www.youtube.com/watch?v=3tJlfj6C0sA. (Accessed on January 25, 2017).

TOTO (2015). *TOTO Corporate Report 2015*. https://jp.toto.com/en/company/profile/library/index.htm. (Accessed on January 25, 2017).

TOTO (2019). *TOTO Group Integrated Report*. from https://jp.toto.com/en/company/profile/library/index.htm. (Accessed on December 25, 2019).

TOTO Corporation (2020). www.toto.com. (Accessed on November 12, 2020).

TOTO Press Releases (2015). *We have a major advantage when it comes to technology*, Interview with Soichi Abe, Director, Managing Executive Officer TOTO. from https://it.toto.com/stampa/press-releases/?no_cache=1&tx_ttnews%5Btt_news%5D=487. (Accessed on January 25, 2020).

TOTO Press Releases (2015). *Toto products are a great fit for hotels*, Interview with Kazuo Sako, Chairman and ECO at TOTO Europe and TOTO USA. https://gb.toto.com/press/press/?tx_ttnews%5Btt_news%5D=519&cHash=e 82b0fcdc346c2a0bc9af965b7b94721. (Accessed on January 25, 2017).

TOTO Press Releases (2013). *Villeroy & Boch and TOTO launch cooperation.* https://gb.toto.com/press/press/?tx_ttnews%5Btt_news%5D=314&cHash=b 769db2d16bd58dd1239b524bbd2a851. (Accessed on January 25, 2020).

© 2021 World Scientific Publishing Company
https://doi.org/10.1142/9789811231032_0011

Case 11

NTT International — Transforming a Japanese Keiretsu into a Tech Giant

Sven Colen

Introduction

In 2017, Barzan Rana commenced working for the "Nippon Telegraph and Telephone" (NTT) Group. The highly respected sales expert made this career move with great ambition, since the Japanese Enterprise had a revenue of over 100 billion USD, a huge player in the information technology and telecommunication industry. He was poached for the exciting mission of establishing the "Extreme Large Deal Organization" (ELDO) as an umbrella organization for all NTT companies in the western world. This strategic and structural bundling of the subsidiaries was supposed to be the next big step in the growth strategy. The goal was to acquire "Extreme Large Deals" (ELD) in the IT industry. In this case, an ELD is defined as an IT outsourcing and consulting project with a volume bigger than a hundred million US Dollars. The scope of an ELD is usually very wide and requires a large variety of IT capabilities. By regularly acquiring some ELDs each year, NTT would push into a new business dimension and would finally belong to the largest IT and technology companies worldwide.

Two years later, while waiting for his flight to Tokyo at Heathrow Airport in London, many different concerning thoughts crossed Barzan Rana's mind. Could he have expected that his mission would be this complex to accomplish in the current company structure? Should he have known the Japanese management methods better in advance? Was it a big mistake to take on this role? After enthusiastically starting to work as Head of Extreme Large Deal Organization, he quickly realized that NTT had sufficient financial resources, technical know-how and worldwide distribution networks, but also that all of these resources are completely dispersed over the different subsidiaries. NTT has grown according to the classical Japanese diversification strategy and is structured after it as of today. Over the past few decades, the company has realized very large company acquisitions, but has not integrated them into the existing corporate structure. After the takeovers, almost no changes were initiated, and most subsidiaries operate almost completely independently as of today. In this structure, ELDO is supposed to acquire ELDs, in which many subsidiaries are required to work closely together for years and across different corporate levels.

In his work so far, Barzan Rana was confronted more so with unsolved problems and challenges than with any pleasing progress. It was very tedious to establish mutual trust, new procedures, structures and functional communication across the different subsidiaries. However, within the next twenty-four hours, he had to present the current state of ELDO and recommendations for the future in front of the Execution Board including the President in the NTT Corporation headquarter in Tokyo.

NTT — A Japanese Keiretsu

NTT was founded originally as a state-owned telecommunication company in 1952, but was privatized in 1985 (NTT Group Website, 2019). The headquarters (HQ) has always been in Tokyo, Japan, and NTT was mainly responsible for the establishment of telecommunication infrastructures in Japan. Today, the corporation operates mostly in the following segments: Long-distance and international communications business, regional communications business, mobile communications business and data communications business. Moreover, the company is highly diversified by also being active in real estate, finance, engineering, system integration and data processing, and development of technologies and shared operations (Forbes, 2019a). According to the Forbes Global 2000, with a revenue of 109.1 billion USD and a profit of 15.6 billion USD (NTT Report, 2019), in 2019, NTT ranked number 51 among the world's largest companies (Forbes, 2019b). NTT employs 303,350 people worldwide.

In order to archive growth, NTT followed mostly the classic Japanese approach of growth strategy — diversification. In Japan, a characteristic of the corporate governance system is cross-shareholding. Many Japanese businesses are part of a large umbrella company, which are called Keiretsu. This is a group of Japanese businesses that are closely linked through reciprocal shareholding and form a strong corporate unit (Collins Dictionary, 2019). Usually, the companies of a Keiretsu are legally independent, but economically dependent on each other (Gabler Lexicon, 2018). Simplified, a Keiretsu is a Japanese mega corporation, which is active in a variety of industries.

The Japanese Corporate Model

In this governance framework, a suitable diversification strategy is required. The diversification is mostly important to explore growth opportunities and to reduce risks (Nishi, 2015). In the strategic process of diversification, Japanese corporations follow the "Industrial Organization" (I/O) model. The I/O model uses an outside approach of evaluating industries for future investments. First, the external environment of many industries is analyzed according to general factors and competitors. Second, an industry gets located with high potential for above-average returns. This means that in this industry, it is likely that an investor can achieve a higher return on the investment compared to the average of other investments. Third, a market entry strategy for the particular industry gets defined. Fourth, necessary assets and skills for entering the chosen industry need to be acquired and developed. Lastly, the firm uses their internal strengths, e.g. resources or capabilities, to execute the strategy (Trumble, 2009).

This external approach of identifying worthwhile market entries into new businesses and industries has greatly accelerated diversification in Japan. Since the I/O model only includes the company's capabilities and resources in the last step of the approach, any attractive business opportunity can be considered for growth. Therefore, Japanese businesses simply discover new profitable opportunities and tackle them. One way of entering these new industries is the acquisition of a company, which is already active in the targeted industry. Thus, in general, Japanese corporations buy many firms.

However, since the Japanese company has little expertise in the new industry, the acquired company can usually simply continue its work and receives only a little influence from its new owner. Mostly, the mother company does not integrate the new subsidiary into a corporate structure or establish any connection between subsidiaries. Moreover, the acquired company often keeps its original name and brands. The top managers stay in their positions and simply receive the goal to maintain their success, growth rate and their profitability. Due to this strategic approach, huge Keiretsus have been generated over the last decades. Each of them includes a high number of independent companies with different names in various industries. One of these mega corporations is NTT.

The resource-based model focuses more on internal perspectives. A company evaluates its own strengths, resources and capabilities first. Afterward, the identification of new interesting markets with the potential of above-average returns, in which the company's strategic resources can be a competitive advantage, begins. Thus, compared to the I/O model, in the resource-based approach, the internal possibilities are more critical than the conditions of the external environment (Barney, 2000).

Global Expansion

In the late 1980s, the original telecommunication company NTT began to extend its portfolio by launching the mobile communication business "NTT Docomo". Moreover, NTT entered the new information technology industry by launching the data communication business "NTT DATA". In 1999, after NTT had been expended to the long-distance international communication business by establishing "NTT Communications", a strong period of diversification began. Through entering a variety of markets, such as real estate, finance, construction/electric power, system development, advanced technology development and more, the company truly became a Keiretsu (NTT Group Website, 2019).

Today, the original regional telecommunications business in Japan reports sales of approximately 29 billion USD, which accounts only for 26.6% of the total revenue (NTT Report, 2019). In particular, this is due to the fact that NTT not only diversified the portfolio to different industries but also started to diversify vertically. For example, in order to strengthen the market position in the international communication business, "Dimension Data" was acquired. More new subsidiaries were launched in different areas of the internet industry, like "NTT Security" and "NTT Research".

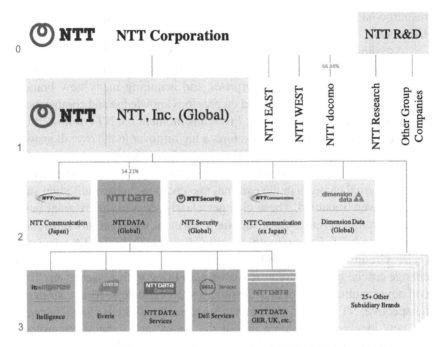

Figure 1. NTT group organigram (based on NTT Ltd. Website, 2019).

In the last 10 years, the subsidiary "NTT DATA", active in the information technology industry, became even a corporation itself by acquiring many companies, including "Everis", "Keane" and "Itelligence". In 2016, "NTT DATA" launched into new dimensions by buying "Dell Services" for approximately 3 billion USD (NTT DATA Website, 2019). All these acquisitions in the last decade led to the complex company structure NTT has today. The current organizational chart is shown in Figure 1.

Growth Challenges

Although NTT has acquired many companies, the corporation does not match all the characteristics of a classical Keiretsu. Especially demonstrated through vertical diversification, NTT tried to develop as a big technology corporation by exploring its own strengths. The management explored growth opportunities in areas where NTT companies already had their own expertise and competencies. This approach follows the resource-based view of Western companies rather than the I/O model of Keiretsus.

As shown above, approximately fifteen years ago, NTT began to expand its market position especially in the information technology industry by launching new enterprises and acquiring many new brands. These strategic actions were based on previous knowledge and competences the corporation already obtained. From this moment on, NTT followed the resource-based model more. Therefore, a big turnover in the overall growth strategy was recognizable around the turn of the millennium.

With the increased importance of brands, NTT also began to make timely internal changes in the external presentation. Some individual subsidiaries were renamed. These changes clearly showed the external business environment (customers, suppliers, partners, etc.) that this subsidiary belonged to NTT. For example, "Keane" became "NTT DATA Services" (NTT Group Website, 2019). However, the top managements did not change crucial internal structures, responsibilities or processes of any firm and never mutually integrated subsidiaries. Nevertheless, from a strategic perspective, NTT strived more and more toward a Western vision, because the new idea was to become one of the largest and greatest technology companies of the world. But, in order to reach this goal, it was indispensable to use synergies and economies of scale. Therefore, it was not sufficient anymore to operate countless smaller businesses. The corporation wanted to establish new businesses across subsidiaries to reach a new revenue level and the top management searched for potential markets big enough to leverage the revenue massively.

After considering the capabilities of the subsidiaries, shown in Figure 2, the choice fell on becoming a global end-to-end IT supplier in the business-to-business industry. With the combined power of the subsidiaries "NTT DATA" (including "Itelligence", "Everis", "NTT DATA Services" and "Dell Services"), "Dimension Data", "NTT Communications" and "NTT Security", NTT had all the capabilities to provide full end-to-end IT support for even the biggest clients in the world. Management consultancy services for future IT strategy development, large digital infrastructure services down to small IT workplace requirements or providing full high-end cyber security, NTT could deal with all IT-related demands of a client. In addition, the size of NTT can be a huge competitive advantage on this market since there are not many companies in the world who can actually deliver end-to-end IT service.

Level	Company	Service Portfolio	Revenue	Business Regions
2	NTT DATA	Consulting, System development and integration, Network system services Business IT outsourcing	20 billion USD (NTT DATA Report, 2019)	Americas, Asian-Pacific, China, Japan, Europe, Middle East
2	Dimension Data	Digital infrastructure (Data centers, network integration, converged communications), Hybrid cloud services, IT workspaces (Microsoft and SAP support), Cybersecurity	8 billion USD (Report Dimension Data, 2018)	Americas, Middle East, Europe Africa, Asia Pacific, Australia
2	NTT Communications (ex. Japan)	International telecommunications operations, Infrastructure Services, Application Services	13 billion USD (NTT Communications Report, 2019)	Americas, Asia-Pacific, Europe
2	NTT Security	Cybersecurity, Workplace Services, Software Implementation	N/A	Americas, Asia-Pacific, Japan, Europe
3	Itelligence	SAP Support, Application Services	1 billion USD (Itelligence Report, 2018)	Middle Europe
3	Everis	Consulting, IT Transformation, Big Data Analytics, AI and Robotics	1,58 billion USD (Everis Report, 2019)	Europe, Americas
3	NTT DATA Services	Application Services, Infrastructure and Business Process Outsourcing	N/A	Europe, Americas
3	Dell Services	Infrastructure Services, IT Workplaces	N/A	Americas, Europe, Middle East

Figure 2. Overview of IT suppliers of NTT companies worldwide.

If the client is big enough, their managers prefer to have only one global IT service provider, because it usually reduces many problems.

Therefore, the new mission was to become a major long-term IT partner for huge projects or whole infrastructures of all possible big clients by winning large IT-planning and outsourcing deals.

This ambitious new mission of transforming NTT into an end-to-end IT supplier for major companies was a very competitive one. In order to become such a long-term and major IT supplier, NTT needed to win ELD.

Usually, big companies assign their IT infrastructure or new big project long-term supplier contracts to a selected supplier. Only one of these contracts can have a budget from 100 million USD to more than one billion USD. Such a deal runs for 5 to 15 years and includes a variety of services. Examples for such projects are the IT support for the entire e-mobility segment of the Daimler AG for the next 10 years or the whole infrastructure supply for every office employee of the Amazon Corporation for the next 12 years. In order to determine the market potential of ELDs, many markets need to be analyzed since ELDs usually combine many of them.

First, one part of an ELD could cover the global technology consulting market, which consists of services of many disciplines. Only this market has a size of 48 billion USD and is growing steadily and strongly (Consultancy.org, 2017). Second, an even bigger business in the information technology industry is the IT outsourcing market, which will also be tackled by acquiring ELDs. This market grew massively in the last 20 years to a size of 88.9 billion USD in 2017 (Statista, 2017). IT outsourcing is to work with external suppliers to handle information technology functions, such as application development, data center operations, workplace support, disaster recovery, help desk, network operations and web hosting (SumatoSoft, 2019).

Third, other market shares in, for example, the business process outsourcing market or the IT security market can be also tackled by winning an ELD.

Extremely Large IT Deal Business

In order to receive a profound picture of the realizability of winning ELDs, it is necessary to take a look at the current major players. The competitors with the most market shares are Accenture, HCL Technologies, Hewlett Packard Enterprise, IBM and Tata Consultancy Services (Market Reports World, 2019). Figure 3 summarizes the key facts. All of these corporations are already well established in the ELD market and can offer an end-to-end IT supply for the entire world. NTT needed to find a suitable strategy and structure to enter this market in order to win ELDs.

Company Name	Company Description	Revenue 2018/19	Employe-es	Business Area
Accenture	Is one of the world's largest management consulting, technology and outsourcing service providers	43.2 billion USD (Consultancy. asia, 2019)	489,000 (Accenture Website, 2019)	Worldwide, HQ in Dublin, Ireland
HCL Technologies	Supplier of Software Consulting, Enterprise Transformation, Decentralized Infrastructure Management, Engineering & R&D Services and Business Process Outsourcing	8.82 billion USD (Ojog, 2019)	120,000 (Forbes, 2019c)	Worldwide, HQ in Noida, India
Hewlett Packard Enterprise	An information technology company focused on servers, network and storage products, IT outsourcing and consulting	30.6 billion USD (Forbes, 2019d)	60,000 (Forbes, 2019d)	Worldwide, HQ in San José, US
IBM	One of the world's leading IT hardware, software and services companies and one of the largest consulting firms.	79.6 billion USD (IBM Report, 2018)	350,600 (IBM Report, 2018)	Worldwide, HQ in Armonk, US
TATA Consultancy Services	A global provider of IT services, consulting and business solutions.	20.9 billion USD (Forbes, 2019e)	400,875 (Forbes, 2019e)	Worldwide, HQ in Mumbai, India

Figure 3.   Overview of competition in the ELD market.

For the top management of NTT in Japan, it was obvious that the acquisition of ELDs would be the biggest challenge, because of the difficult competition. At the time, they did not care too much about the actual delivery of the services, since the subsidiaries combined had more than enough skills and expertise to handle all possible client demands. Therefore, they started to search for an efficient structure for establishing a sales department which only focused on acquiring ELDs. In addition, they searched for suitable candidates with expertise and experience in this area. In this instance, NTT was successful in hiring Barzan Rana in 2017.

He was considered a successful and experienced dealmaker for ELDs and had already been working for more than twenty years in this area. He was highly motivated for his new position because of the aspiration of this huge project and the vision behind it.

In consultation with the top management of NTT in Europe, he suggested that it would not be sufficient to establish only a new department in one of the subsidiaries. Instead, his new business unit must be easily approachable for all subsidiaries and able to act neutrally as well as completely transparently in the corporation. Thus, in agreement with the NTT board in Tokyo, they decided to establish a new umbrella organization for all subsidiaries and called it the "Extreme Large Deal Organization" (ELDO). From an organizational perspective, ELDO was thereby not part of any subsidiary. It was a direct, extended arm of NTT from Japan. Barzan Rana had been appointed Vice President and Head of ELDO and was directly subordinate to the Head of Global Business and a Board Member of NTT. In addition, he had to report to all global CEOs of the most important subsidiaries. From this moment on, he was fully responsible for the establishment of the ELDO. Figure 4 shows the organizational integration of ELDO into NTT.

After creating the organizational unit, Barzan Rana created a simple vision for ELDO:

"ELDO aims to acquire ELDs with a minimum volume of 100 million USD." At the beginning, the focus was placed on Europe and the Middle East, but later, on the entire world.

In order to work efficiently, ELDO was divided into two areas of action, deal management and bid management. In the deal management section were the dealmakers, who were responsible for finding new ELDs and bringing them into the bid stage. In this phase, the bid management overtakes the deal responsibility. A bid is basically the offer from a company on realizing a deal. In ELDs, a bid is a very long and complex process since one has to determine a scope for the deal, responsibilities, prices and more. The presentations of the offers are also part of the bid process and, in most cases, due diligence is a part of the bid process, too. Depending on the size of the deal, the bid process can last up to two years.

Barzan Rana began to work in both areas in parallel. Although he had already built such structures in another company, he quickly encountered big problems and resistance in both areas of action.

In terms of the deal management, Barzan Rana recognized in the initial events with potential clients that NTT was not known as an end-to-end IT

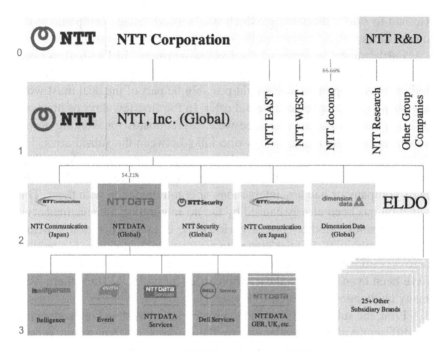

Figure 4. ELDO integration into NTT.

service provider. The brand was much better known as a telecommunications company. Moreover, the representatives of potential clients were skeptical that NTT had enough capabilities for delivering an ELD. In fact, they did not know that companies like Dimension Data were also part of the NTT corporation. Through the Japanese style of managing subsidiaries by leaving their brand names untouched, it was simply incomprehensible for outsiders to recognize the actual size of the NTT. Thus, ELDO had to start at the roots of marketing and sales by establishing recognizability and awareness that NTT is indeed capable of managing ELDs.

Moreover, the dealmakers recognized that they must create a deal pipeline. Since ELDs are huge and long-term businesses, new ELD opportunities do not appear very often. In fact, timing is very important. Thus, ELDO must constantly monitor the market in order to be ready and in place at the right time for an ELD. A deal pipeline, in which contacts and deal possibilities arise overseas on a regular basis, would be such a monitoring system. Unfortunately, Barzan Rana did not find any kind of a monitoring system on the global stage in any of the NTT subsidiaries.

He had to start with nothing, which was a disadvantage compared to the competitors.

Furthermore, in terms of the bid management, ELDO had to overcome even bigger challenges. In order to create an efficient and effective bid process, all parties who would possibly be part of the deal must work together to create a reasonable bid offer. In the first few days of his work at NTT, Barzan Rana recognized weak prerequisites for working across subsidiaries — there were almost no links between the subsidiaries. The companies all functioned as entirely independent companies. Apart from the boards, almost no employee had ever worked together with another NTT company or had any interactions or communication with them. This situation has been clearly caused by the no-integration management style of the Japanese mother company. However, in this corporation structure and atmosphere, ELDO has started to create a highly complex bid process across continents and subsidiaries. Without this process, NTT would not have been even able to make a simple offer for an ELD. Thus, there were many challenges to overcome (Figure 4).

First, the subsidiaries needed to create mutual trust and understanding on different company levels. Among the workers, awareness and knowledge of each other was needed. It was necessary for managers to understand the goals, values and strengths of the other subsidiaries, and it was essential for the top management to commit themselves to new strategic goals, which are broader than any previous focused goals.

Second, a new cross-subsidiary procedure framework needed to be established and supported by all parties. A bid process usually goes through a variety of approval stages and the bid process cannot proceed before receiving particular approvals. Very often, such approvals are related to investments and costs, for example, offering this price for this specific service or using particular resources for this deal. But, in order to hand out these kinds of approvals, somebody must be authorized to decide on such matters. However, because of the corporation structure, nobody from any of the subsidiaries was authorized to decide on cross-subsidiary questions. Actually, every single small decision would have been made by the HQ in Japan, which was obviously impossible.

Third, the most important factor to win an ELD, except the network of the dealmaker, is mostly the offered price. But, NTT struggled greatly, especially in this aspect, since there was no joint price management system in place across subsidiaries. Usually, by bidding on an ELD, the IT supplier submits one final price. In order to create one common price for all services across the subsidiaries, ELDO must have asked each subsidiary to submit an offer for their requested services. Afterward, ELDO could have added up all different offers to one final price. But, since all different price offers of the subsidiaries consisted of buffers and margins, the final price would have been much too high to have any chance of actually winning the ELD against the competition. This final price would not include any synergies and economies of scale. ELDO had the problem that none of the subsidiaries would have been willing to renounce their margin. Moreover, in many cases, it could even be that some subsidiaries lose money with a deal and just NTT as a whole makes a profit out of the deal. However, no manager would have ever supported such deals in the current corporation structure. Moreover, they would have most likely tried to prevent them.

Lastly, ELDO did not have any authorized power to change such high-level structures or strategies. Rather, the opposite was the case. From a political perspective, it would have been very dangerous for ELDO to try and influence these high-level management decisions, because managers are usually very sensitive about keeping control of their powers. Such changes could have only been made by an active influence from the HQ in Tokyo, which would have been completely against the Japanese way of managing subsidiaries.

In conclusion, ELDO was starting to establish mutual trust, communication and commitment between the subsidiaries and create external awareness that NTT is transforming into a big player in the ELD market. However, ELDO was confronted with many problems. Nonetheless, the HQ expected measurable success from ELDO since they invested a lot of money in it. Struggling with the described challenges and under enormous pressure, Barzan Rana had to travel to the HQ in Tokyo now. In twenty-four hours, he had to make a presentation over the current state of ELDO and his recommendations for the future in front of the Executive Board of NTT.

Questions

1. What is the idea behind NTT and what are they trying to achieve with ELDO?
2. What are the key challenges for ELDO to overcome? Which problems might arise for ELDO due to the Japanese organizational culture and management style?

3. What are the possible solutions to overcome the described challenges?
4. What kind of support will ELDO need from the NTT board to achieve the goal?

References

Accenture Website, (2019). About Accenture. Available at: https://www.accenture.com/us-en/about/company-index (Accessed on December 7, 2019).

Barney, J.B. (2000). Firm resources and sustained competitive advantage, in: *Journal of Management*, 17(1), pp. 99–120.

Collins Dictionary (2019). Keiretsu definition and meaning | Collins English Dictionary. Available at: https://www.collinsdictionary.com/dictionary/english/keiretsu (Accessed on January 16, 2020).

Consultancy.asia (2019). Accenture pushes global revenues to $43.2 billion for 2019. https://tinyurl.com/y6vjthd5 (Accessed on January 16, 2020).

Consultancy.org (2017). IT Consulting. Available at: https://www.consultancy.org/consulting-industry/it-consulting (Accessed on December 17, 2019).

Everis Report (2019). Everis increases its revenue by 22% and reaches EUR 1.43 billion. //www.everis.com/global/en/news/newsroom/everis-increases-revenue-143-billion (Accessed on December 17, 2019).

Forbes (2019a). Nippon Telegraph & Tel on the Forbes Global 2000 List. Forbes. https://www.forbes.com/companies/nippon-tel-tel/ (Accessed on December 5, 2019).

Forbes (2019b). Global 2000 — The World's Largest Public Companies 2019. Forbes. https://www.forbes.com/global2000/ (Accessed on December 5, 2019).

Forbes (2019c). HCL Technologies. Forbes. https://www.forbes.com/companies/hcl-technologies/?sh=2a942653e93f (January 16, 2020).

Forbes (2019d). Hewlett Packard Enterprise. Forbes. https://www.forbes.com/companies/hewlett-packard-enterprise/ (Accessed on December 16, 2020).

Forbes (2019e). Tata Consultancy Services. Forbes. https://www.forbes.com/companies/tata-consultancy-services/?sh=42ba2dd71966 (Accessed on January 16, 2020).

Gabler Lexicon (2018). Keiretsu • Definition | Gabler Wirtschaftslexikon. https://wirtschaftslexikon.gabler.de/definition/keiretsu-36961 (Accessed on January 16, 2020).

IBM Report (2018). IBM_Annual_Report_2018. Available at: https://www.ibm.com/annualreport/assets/downloads/IBM_Annual_Report_2018.pdf (Accessed on January 16, 2020).

Itelligence Report (2018). Itelligence: Unternehmensnews und Informationen. Itelligence Deutschland. Available at: https://itelligencegroup.com/de/presse/ (Accessed on December 17, 2019).

Market Reports World (2019). IT Outsourcing Market 2019 Global Industry Size, Revenue Growth Development, Business Opportunities, Future Trends, Top Key Players, Market Share and Global Analysis by Forecast to 2022. MarketWatch. https://tinyurl.com/y8opycb7 (Accessed on December 17, 2019).

Nishi, T. (2015). Corporate diversification and board composition in Japanese electronics corporations. *International Journal of Business and Management*, 3(2), pp. 27–44.

NTT Communications Report (2019). News released by NTT Communications. https://www.ntt.com/en/about-us/press-releases/news/article/2019/0510. html (Accessed on December 7, 2019).

NTT DATA Report (2019). NTT Data Annual Report 2019.

NTT DATA Website (2019). NTT DATA History. NTT DATA. https://tinyurl. com/ybj3wnma (Accessed on December 6, 2019).

NTT Group Website (2019). Our History. Available at: https://www.ntt.co.jp/ index_e.html (Accessed on December 5, 2019).

NTT Ltd. Website (2019). NTT Group. Available at: https://www.global.ntt/ en-us/about-us/ntt-group (Accessed on December 6, 2019).

NTT Report (2019). NTT HOME > To Investors > Financial Data > Financial Highlights. Available at: https://www.ntt.co.jp/ir/fin_e/highlight.html (Accessed on December 5, 2019).

Ojog, O. (2019). HCL Technologies reported financial results for the fourth quarter and fiscal year 2019 | PAC — a teknowlogy Group company. https:// www.sitsi.com/hcl-technologies-reported-financial-results-fourth-quarter- and-fiscal-year-2019 (Accessed on December 16, 2019).

Report Dimension Data (2018). People, Planet and ProfiStatista, 2017. Größte Internetunternehmen nach Börsenwert weltweit 2017 | Statistik. Statista. Available at: https://de.statista.com/statistik/daten/studie/217485/umfrage/ marktwert-der-groessten-internet-firmen-weltweit/ (Accessed on December 6, 2019).

SumatoSoft (2019). IT Outsourcing 2019 Overview & Trends. Medium. https:// medium.com/@sumatosoft/it-outsourcing-2019-overview-trends-8e14744ebf77 (Accessed on December 7, 2019).

Trumble, R. (2009). The I/O Model of Above-Average Returns. https://www. coursehero.com/file/5677019/434-Exam-1/ (Accessed on December 16, 2020).

© 2021 World Scientific Publishing Company
https://doi.org/10.1142/9789811231032_0012

Case 12

Losing Some Steam: Valve

Isaac Kim

Valve

Gabe Newell, colloquially surnamed Gaben, is the founder and CEO of the video game development and digital distribution company Valve, and formerly a Microsoft employee — a man who naturally accumulated fame over time in the young and often tumultuous gaming industry. For the previous 20 years, this sector has been gaining steam and turned out to be a massively profitable discipline, with a focus on younger but easily accessible and international market segments and a wide range of "genres" to develop or discover.

Valve initially only developed computer video game software back in 1998, starting with one called "Half-Life", which turned out to be a massive commercial success, something extremely rare for a debut product. Capitalizing on the initial impetus, the smaller independent company continued to release hit after hit for the next eight or so years. It is in 2003 that they finally developed Steam, first described as a digital software distribution platform integrating most of their previous works for self-promotion and ease of access. They soon shared the platform with outside developers, largely increasing the list of available software. Soon after, it became apparent that publishing third-party products in their storefront and obtaining cuts on sales was a more profitable and easy-to-manage business profile than developing games by themselves, despite the occasional releases, long awaited by ardent fans. Other playing factors were

159

the known limitations of distributing only physical copies: digital piracy, competition with console platforms and the need for frequent online-provided updates to more and more complex gaming software (Adaptive Cycle, 2020).

Steam — Market Leader

Although many other platforms can be seen today, Steam remains by far the largest and most popular: According to Fenlon (2019), Steam's number of users reaches a monthly 90 million, with simultaneous connected users peaking to an all-time high of 18.5 million in 2018 (Gough, 2019). This is mainly due to their aforementioned third-party developer participation system, allowing large companies to let their games be published and maintained with close to no release cost, or even smaller ambitious developers having mainstream access to an enormous user base. Steam also provides an array of additional services, ranging from a simple but efficient enough rating system allowing any customer to post their own reviews (the term "to curate" is often used), a push to buyer power that is much appreciated by the users, to online discussion boards, allowing participants to directly communicate with the product developers themselves.

Within the goal of overcoming their own obstacles, Valve pioneered with their innovative computer game distribution platform. Game sales revenue on Steam was reportedly USD 375.6 million in 2016, exponentially rising to $4.3 billion at the end of the next year, 2017. Other bigger firms in the market knew better than to attempt to challenge Valve's unprecedented monopoly, and instead sectored their own products behind their own "Game launchers". The only two exceptions are Polish CD Projekt-owned GOG.com, which focuses on publishing older, retro games as well as their own mother company's software, followed by Chinese titan Tencent-controlled Epic Games, the biggest external threat Valve will have to face in the coming business years.

Defining the Customer Base

The video game industry works in a significantly different way compared to other forms of entertainment. Retroactive revision on products and consistent support service after release are expected. This instead can be used by developers to distribute prototype versions to a select few, called beta (version) testers, allowing early customer feedback and product testing. In many cases, however, either due to time or financial constraints, unpolished versions are released to the public at full price (which usually range from $20 to more often $80) to guarantee sales. Following these are "patches": post-release versions of the software that are meant to address previous issues. As this software is purely a virtual product, these changes can be applied *en masse* online, greatly streamlining the process. Unsurprisingly, firms prefer to cut as many corners as they are given, as customer dissatisfaction can easily be dispelled in the few days following an initial release. While this is becoming more and more of a common occurrence, it is generally not a good idea to ride the slope of underestimating one's customer base. This is especially the case with the entertainment industry where buyer power and a plethora of competitors can quickly sink a business which has run out of favor in the eye of the clientele. Certain companies who adopted the "half-bake and sell" strategy indeed felt the brunt of it, accumulating poor critic scores, poorer sales and loss of trust.

Another important nuance that should be underlined is player loyalty. Company brand image, alongside the quality of their games, goes a long way in defining customer retention and subsequent product sales, not unlike what defining the style and the popularity of a film director do for his movies.

While more traditional industries can still rely on diverse marketing methods, it would seem video game-related products simply cannot be dissociated from internet culture and savvy. In recent years, this new sphere of entertainment has been simultaneously gaining momentum and increasing its scope of broadcast and advertisement, such as "pro-player" competitions taking place for various games and platforms alike, with the biggest prize pool so far being for Dota 2 (a game developed by Valve), culminating to $30 million for the winning team (Kaser, 2019). These tournaments are organized in a way akin to sports competitions, with professional presenters at its helm, a roaring live public, ornate trophies and well-paying sponsors.

The main way for gaming companies to generate interest, however, is through international conventions hosted around the world, where they can present upcoming titles, or even announce their goals, visions and prospects directly to consumers. The largest are E3 (Electronic Entertainment Expo), TGS (Tokyo Game Show) and Pax.

Gateway to the West

Japan has the longest history in the gaming industry. Many of its older companies are very successful today. Unlike the West, however, many of its consumers and developers alike preferred console platforms as opposed to computer games, with one of the earliest being Nintendo's Famicom, or Family Computer gaming system. Among the "Big Three" platforms that own the majority of the console gaming market shares, two are of Japanese origin, with the primary one being Sony's Playstation, followed from afar by Nintendo's various family-oriented television consoles and handheld devices, and finally the US-made Microsoft Xbox. Despite the focus on battling for their spot in the customers' living rooms, many firms prefer not to remain loyal to a single party (often referred to as "exclusives"), but to broaden their horizons and offer cross-platform sales, or in most cases, expand toward the PC gaming segments.

That is where Steam came into play. Porting games meant for consoles to computer support can be arduous, especially when it comes to redistribution of physical copies. Valve's distribution platform provided the ideal solution. With the domestic Japanese PC games market initially being too small to justify the expansion, Steam's user base, being composed of mainly western players (of the $4.3 billion revenue, 34% North American sales and 29% Western European, according to 2017 Valve statistics), turned out to be a blessing, as any Japanese developer could easily connect with foreign markets through Steam.

Not all of it is easy profits, however, as Japanese games, having a radically different "niche" flavor from what Western players are used to, only really attract a dedicated handful compared to the large number of potential customers (Byford, 2014).

A few studios managed to pull out larger numbers of foreign shares compared to domestic ones by specifically giving their games a more familiar theme and elements. For example, FromSoftware's franchise holds a total of close to 10 million digital copy sales on Steam since its primary release in 2012 with each of the games boasting an impressive shelf life (Figure 1).

Other smaller Japanese companies still struggle to attract more followers. Some attempt to mimic FromSoftware's license by developing products with similar gameplay, but without a real grasp on what made those games so popular among western fandoms, bringing meek revenues and average scores.

Japanese games used to be the trendsetter in the industry's foundational years, since the first arcade games back in 1970. Sony and Nintendo aside, however, many of the country's bigger firms either went bankrupt or switched their focus to other forms of entertainment. The advent of "Competitive Gaming", and the many American companies responsible for its rise in popularity, was another blow for local developers. Beddis (2018) holds the country in a positive light, as Japan is reportedly the third-largest market, and generates over $14 million a year in revenues.

With all that in mind, it does not seem that other Japanese game-developing companies will lose any more steam in the coming years, especially with such ease of access to the West through digital distribution platforms. The main question is if they will manage to exploit that potential and successfully attract more customers, or if they are content with keeping buyers abroad as a secondary source of revenue while prioritizing domestic clientele.

FromSoftware's recent streak of game awards tells the tale of success in foreign segments being perfectly possible. Generating long-term profits mainly hangs on the good quality and game style. Valve Corporation fortunately provides many functions that can help with those two

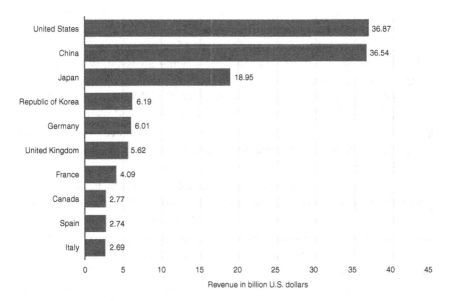

Figure 1.   Leading gaming markets worldwide 2019, by revenue (in billion US$).

qualifications for developers thanks to its freely accessible analytics and close contact with customers in terms of feedback and demands.

With the recent streak of success by Nippon's software production veterans, more and more previously unrelated segment clusters start to turn their eyes toward the eastern side of the industry, opening the gates to a new clientele, and Steam seems to be the highway to reach their wallet. Rather than leaving its Steam customer base on the back burner, many Japanese companies might consider having a closer look at potential annual sales on the platform and rearranging their market segment priority. This, of course, is not without risks, given the necessary efforts to shift their style of products, and adapt to Western demands.

The Situation

Valve had received a revenue of $4.3 billion from Steam sales in 2017, about $800 million more than its previous year's estimations. Despite the rising numbers, the company's progress chart starts to show a few dents.

According to Cornell (2018), Valve's main recipe for global success can be attributed to its company structure and management style, which promote creative flow and favor diversity in iteration.

Steam seemingly hit its peak between January and October 2018, with an estimated 18.5 million concurrent users. Gough (2019) reports a downward trend in numbers ever since, to 14.15 million toward the end of 2019. Rather than Valve's platform itself being an issue, the shared yet distant Console game segments of the gaming industry has been continuously taking parts out of Valve's own consumer shares: Release of new consoles promising better support for more complex and well-made game products, and many of the latter announced as "Exclusive" to designated platform meant more and more of the laptop and desktop crowd attracted to the living room space.

In 2015, Valve launched its own Steam Controller, a configurable joint hardware and software that mimics the features of a console with the possibility to play games from a user's Steam library on television with said controller. The product ended up being a failed venture, albeit with much capital to recoup the losses on Valve's part. Valve's flat and less strict management structure is and has been the main obstacle for the software to hardware manufacturing transition, resulting in an overall lesser quality product, more so should it be compared to its veteran console competitors (Cornell, 2018).

Figure 2. Overview global games market (Macdonald, 2017).

Issues other than internal ones can also be attributed to the "machine failure", however, as Statt (2018) suggests: Steam appealed to a specific player base that would prefer using computers as a gaming support due to several irreplaceable reasons, such as configurability of hardware, with graphic cards, screen size or available RAM being largely reliant on a customer's wallet depth, but also being an important freedom of choice. One of the more interesting parts is the fact that mouse and keyboard is favored as being more reliable and precise than their controller counterparts, and the majority of PC players would hardly part with it. Those who prefer controllers also have the choice to plug and play with one on their computer, depending on the software (Figure 2).

Hence, the Steam hardware category of products was, at best, a rather blind and half-hearted attempt at penetrating the console market all the while trying to keep its library computer-oriented (Wales, 2019). A justified decision after all, as Valve not exploiting what Steam is best known for would have come out as a waste. But, Valve's lack of motivation and inexperience in the hardware domain has proven to be the primary issue.

With its strong partnerships with concurrent game giants Electronic Arts and especially Acer, giving the helm to a subsidiary for manufacturing might have provided better results in terms of product quality for the

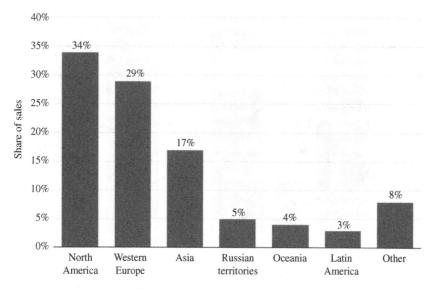

Figure 3.   Steam sales by region (Gough, 2017).

Steam controller, while letting internal teams focus on providing the best possible support for the computer-to-television support shift. Marketing and segment targeting would also have played an important role.

Analyst Christina Gough on Statista (2017) expresses doubt concerning Valve's continuous success, yet the company still holds a few cards in hand. It is only a matter of making the right move at the right time.

Newfound threat in familiar waters

Console gaming is not the only offensive launched against Valve. In recent years, Tencent Holding Limited, a Shenzhen-based Chinese multinational, has been a looming threat. Tencent's game division has been acquiring the rights of many popular game studios, such as Riot Games, a younger company with a massive hit product called League of Legend, a competitive multiplayer team game still enjoyed today and continuously holding internationally broadcasted tournaments.

Any game company that wishes to enter the massive Chinese market requires partnership with Tencent in some way or another. This is not limited to computer game producers; Nintendo has been in partnership with Tencent to introduce the Switch in China (Gilbert, 2019).

More importantly, Tencent owns a substantial part of stakes in Epic Games, the company responsible for creating Fortnite, currently the most-played game in the world (Giret, 2019) with over 250 million players.

Interestingly, Fortnite's main but smaller competitor is another game called PUBG, sponsored by and sold on Steam, boasting a grand total of 400 million players worldwide. Yet, with Fortnite as its muscles, like Alexander the Great invading the massive Persian Empire, Epic Games challenged the computer gaming giant on its home ground with a familiar yet surprising strategy.

Battle for market shares

In December 2018, Epic Games announced its own appropriately named Epic Games Store, a digital distribution platform with integrated launcher similar to Steam. So far, the main competitive strategy Epic Games has employed is one akin to how console platforms have been securing grounds — exclusivity to their own platform for popular computer game releases.

Epic Games promises hefty sums to developers signing their time-exclusive contracts. Their game is to be released solely on the Epic Games Store for a few years until its popularity naturally turns stale, according to Bardwell (2019). This is exceedingly tempting for small to medium-sized firms, as on top of the contractual payment, Epic Games also benefits by only 12% of the profits from developers, as opposed to Steam which would take a full 30% cut. Given the financial conditions offered by Epic Games, there would be little to no reasons for most studios not to accept the deal. After all, the exclusivity contract provides much-needed financial security to firms in the domain, as many had to close their doors due to poor sales in this unpredictable market (Asarch, 2019).

The catch is that they would not be allowed to publish their games on any other domains. While this may not seem very relevant for digital products at first glance, players have developed a certain form of identity based on what the company stands for. Many have strong loyalty toward Steam in the computer entertainment sector. Potential buyers expressed negativity toward the "lock-out" contract by Epic Games, declaring they would rather wait a few years until the exclusivity period is over than contributing to the scheme, a practice they call "voting with your wallet". This in turn may not bode well for potential partners, as while Epic games provide an upfront

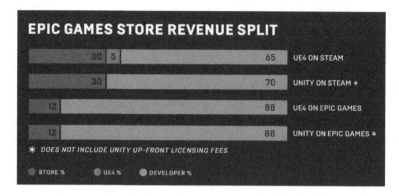

Figure 4.   Revenues of epic games (Yamanaka, 2018).

payment to any contractors, failing to recoup their own production costs guarantees no further support from Tencent's American satellite firm.

The controversy, however, has not stopped many major and minor developer studios from joining the swelling ranks of Epic's exclusivity scheme. Ahmad (2019) quoted Digital Bros receiving €9.49 million in payment for a single software. Tim Sweeney, founder and CEO of Epic Games, expects there will be no more need to approach developers themselves for a one-to-one contract, but many others attracted by the satisfying sales figures and financial backing will eventually join by themselves.

So far, Valve has been oddly silent regarding Epic Game's sudden invasive strategy. Parts of the customer base assume they are simply preparing similarly enticing terms for developers to (re)join their platform as a means to counteract their newfound competitor's costly measures, but there has not been an announcement or any data leaks indicating as such. Many others predict that, while Steam indubitably reigns as the king of the hill in the computer games segment, their current position also limits their capacity to switch gears or adapt to sudden changes in trends. That much is confirmed, given the responsibility Valve has toward its numerous stakeholders, unlike Epic Games backed by the giant Tencent.

The aforementioned delve into Valve's inner management style indicates difficulty in keeping an uptight and precise flow for operations. Their rather flat hierarchy as well as cronyism/favoritism playing an ultimately stronger argument regarding positions led to the corporation struggling to revitalize with other less indulgent companies in terms of efficiency, hardware development or massive goal shifts, one that may be required to protect Valve's interests against the "platform exclusivity plague".

But, it is that same lax management style paired with promotion of artistic flow that allowed Valve to rise to such degrees. Their proximity with clients, apparent generosity with seasonal product sales (well known in the domain as "Steam Sales") and excellent global reputation proportionally to their user base size made them fan favorites. With that said, Epic Games' increasing exclusive games library still convinced many of their loyalists to come and favor the franchises now "held hostage" by the former, which, instead of mimicking the Steam Sales promotion, decided to give out entirely free copies of games offered every month. Strickland (2019) reported over 85 million users in the Epic Store, a significant milestone given the infant stage the platform is currently developing through.

Virtual Reality Games — The Next Hype?

An interesting trend that can be seen on Steam's main page is its increasing tilt toward virtual reality-related software promotion (Figure 5). Virtual Reality (VR) goggles provide its owners the possibility to explore

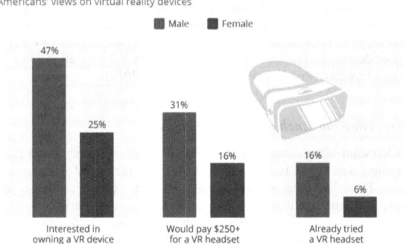

Figure 5.   Future of virtual reality (Richter, 2016a).

virtual spaces in a 3-dimensional environment complete with near direct interaction thanks to its motion-detecting controllers in each hand. Developers and players alike believe VR to be the next generation of entertainment, although, the claims are still too flimsy to be taken for granted. This high-end piece of hardware costs $600 on average, double the price of the popular Nintendo Switch console on its own. Its overall performance is less than stellar compared to what one can imagine virtual games could be like, and the amount of games currently available on the platform is limited. Valve intended to remedy that.

More than 4.7 million VR headsets were sold at the beginning of the year (Hoium, 2019), and the prices seem to have dropped further mid-2019; all the while, technological improvements for each headset are delivered version upon version.

Helping promote virtual reality software developers on Steam, it would seem that Valve is attempting to set the trends in the industry toward the "future of gaming". The king of the hill has already bid much of its funds in anticipation, encouraging third-party studios to collaborate. These elaborate machines cannot run on their own, however, and require to be linked to a computer providing the horsepower necessary to run most of the complex interactive software. This is where Steam VR comes in, a free secondary platform that helps the computer run the game and essentially "links" it to the headset. With many of the game enthusiasts being already familiar with Steam, the transition was smooth and the user base quickly grew since its launch. Even the VR headset pioneer HTC in Taiwan uses Steam VR as its main support. Interestingly, this puts HTC in a difficult position as Valve has also decided to relaunch hardware equipment despite its previous failures, this time in VR as well, selling for much less than what HTC could offer (Hoium, 2019).

Expecting too much of an infant industry

A keyword often associated with Virtual reality is "barebones": Basic features were found lacking and controls inside the virtual space are riggity. There has been massive investment from venture capitalists and abundant promises from both tech celebrities such as Mark Zuckerberg and hardware developers alike. According to Roe (2019), the Global Mixed Reality market might reach the $2.3 billion mark by 2023. VR, unfortunately, still has a long way to go before becoming a mainstream form of entertainment among the clientele. Opinions are highly divided as to when this gadget will take its place in the average consumer's living room, yet they all point toward the same answer: We do not know.

There is little skepticism regarding the VR industry as a power player in the future, but it is very possible that, by the time all these investments bear fruit and VR finally generates enough traction and revenue alike, opportunity cost and decay would have rendered them null and void.

Recent Fortune's article (Aric Jenkins, 2019) argues that it is a mind-blowing experience, worth every penny it requires to have it in your hands (and face), but concludes that the last but indubitably hardest step is to fully convince hundreds of millions of other potential buyers.

Despite Valve's efforts to promote and support the "logical next step" for not only games but human experience in general, the uncertainty of when the industry will find a beachhead to the majority of the market implies Gabe Newell will have to find a sound bridge to cross to the next generation of entertainment.

No high road to success

With Epic Games gaining ground and the relentless console games company locking Valve out of major amounts of shares, the makers of Steam are compelled to find alternative ways to maintain their dominion over the shrinking PC games market until Virtual Reality can take the lead. In an attempt to ease the transition, Valve had announced in 2019 a sequel to Half-Life, the game that first propelled the company to such heights of popularity in the first place. This time, however, the software would be a VR exclusive. While there is no doubt many ardent fans of Valve games who have been waiting for a new release for so long might find reasons enough to purchase a headset, similar to how devoted players buy new consoles solely for a single exclusive product, the requirements might have an adverse effect on the rest of the customers.

There is no saying what Valve's plans are for the future: either spurning a computer-focused platform philosophy and setting all sails toward the ever-grossing Global Mixed Reality market (which, according to Roe (2019), may boast a consistent 77.3% growth rate up to 2023), or taking a softer approach and slowly converting its user base toward VR usage, a very realistic hypothesis given the firm's homebrewed engine and hardware products already available in the market.

While Epic Games or even Nintendo (outside of Nintendo Labo) have not revealed any solid plans of shifting focus to VR themselves, Valve should ensure their competitors do not come chasing them down. Giving Epic a taste of its own medicine by holding on to successful VR developers in the future by means of an exclusivity contract is a simple solution.

The Future of VR

An important detail Valve should have ingrained in the back of their management's minds is that the use of virtual or augmented reality extends way beyond simple entertainment. In recent years, more and more veteran and start-up companies alike have offered personalized VR sessions for a variety of real-like tasks (Figure 6).

Information Age's Writer Kayla Matthews (2019) reports that many major companies in all sorts of industries already make use of these

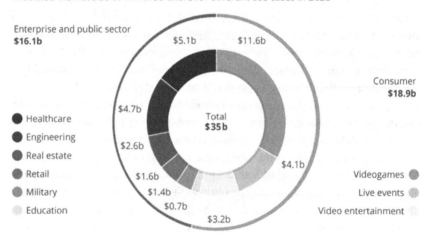

Figure 6.   Predicted markets for virtual reality technology (Richter, 2016b).

futuristic headgears for both personnel and customer usage: Test drive by Volvo, customer service training by Walmart or even fashion runway shows by TopShop. Outside of business practices, public sectors across the globe have found VR and AR to be great training tools for firemen, air force pilots or police officers.

With this in mind, Valve might consider expanding their expertise in VR to more than just entertainment. This might be the opportunity to greatly broaden their horizons by dabbling in multiple markets rather than attempting to sustain leadership inside the ever-limited computer games sector. While the massive upscale in clientele and tech requirements this will demand might be concerning, Gabe Newell's game development company jumped from video game development to worldwide digital support platform and finally to hardware, proving that Valve's peculiarly fluid management style could adapt to both internal and external changes with a certain ease.

References

Adaptive Cycle (2020). *The Dynamic History of Valve. From Game Developer to Console Manufacturer.* http://www.adaptivecycle.nl/images/Mini_case_study_Valve.pdf (Accessed on August 4, 2020).

Asarch, S. (2019). *Is Epic Games Store Exclusivity Worth The Risk? Developers Share Their Stories.* https://www.newsweek.com/epic-games-store-exclusive-developer-game-1456621. (Accessed on August 4, 2020).

Bardwell, T. (2019). *Epic Games Store Exclusivity: You Hate It — Here's Why Developers Don't.* https://www.ccn.com/epic-games-store-exclusivity/. (Accessed on August 4, 2020).

Beddis (2018). *Is Japan Still Setting the Trends in the Gaming Industry?* https://www.hadean.com/blog/is-japan-still-setting-the-trends-in-the-gaming-industry. (Accessed on August 4, 2020).

Byford, S. (2014). *Japan Used to Rule Video Games, So What Happened?* https://www.theverge.com/2014/3/20/5522320/final-fight-can-japans-gaming-industry-be-saved. (Accessed on August 4, 2020).

Cornell University (2018). *Case 5 — Valve Case Study.* https://www.studocu.com/en/document/cornell-university/introduction-to-business-management/mandatory-assignments/case-5-valve-case-study/4212202/view (Accessed on August 4, 2020).

Gilbert, B. (2019). *The Biggest Game Company in the World isn't Nintendo — It's a Chinese Company That has a Piece of Everything from 'Fortnite' to 'League of Legends'*. https://www.businessinsider.in/the-biggest-game-company-in-the-world-isnt-nintendo-160its-a-chinese-company-that-has-a-piece-of-everything-from-fortnite-to-league-of-legends/articleshow/70850159.cms. (Accessed on August 4, 2020).

Gough, C. (2017). Distribution of steam sales revenue worldwide as of August 2017, by region https://www.statista.com/statistics/733320/steam-sales-share-by-region/. (Accessed on November 12, 2020).

Gough, C. (2019). *Number of Peak Concurrent Steam Users from November 2012 to September 2019.* https://www.statista.com/statistics/308330/number-stream-users/. (Accessed on August 4, 2020).

Hoium, T. (2019). *What You Need to Know About Investing in Virtual Reality Technology.* https://www.fool.com/investing/2019/08/27/need-to-know-investing-in-virtual-reality-tech.aspx. (Accessed on August 4, 2020).

Jenkins, A. (2019). *The Fall and Rise of VR: The Struggle to Make Virtual Reality Get Real.* https://fortune.com/longform/virtual-reality-struggle-hope-vr/. (Accessed on August 4, 2020).

Kaser, R. (2019). *Dota 2 International prize pool surpasses $30M, becomes largest in esports history.* https://thenextweb.com/gaming/2019/07/22/dota-2-international-prize-pool30m-becomes-largest-esports-history/. (Accessed on August 4, 2020).

Macdonald, E. (2017). Tom Wijman (2018) *Mobile Revenues Account for More Than 50% of the Global Games Market as It Reaches $137.9 Billion in 2018.* https://newzoo.com/insights/articles/the-global-games-market-will-reach-108-9-billion-in-2017-with-mobile-taking-42/. (Accessed on August 4, 2020).

Matthews, K. (2019). *6 use cases of brands applying VR to their business strategies* [online] Source: https://www.information-age.com/brands-vr-business-strategies-123484738/#. (Accessed on August 4, 2020).

Omerovic, S. (2019). Steam now has more than 90 million active monthly users. https://www.altchar.com/game-news/valve-shares-steam-numbers-90m-monthly-in-2018-a0p2D2x38dlw. (Accessed on August 4, 2020).

Richter, F. (2016a). Is Virtual Reality The Next Big Thing?. https://www.statista.com/chart/4522/consumer-interest-in-virtual-reality/. (Accessed on August 4, 2020).

Richter, F. (2016b). The Diverse Potential of VR & AR Applications. https://www.statista.com/chart/4602/virtual-and-augmented-reality-software-revenue/. (Accessed on August 4, 2020).

Roe, D. (2019). *AR and VR Could Be Mainstream Sooner Than You Think.* https://www.cmswire.com/customer-experience/ar-and-vr-could-be-mainstream-sooner-than-you-think/. (Accessed on August 4, 2020).

Statista (2017). https://www.statista.com/statistics/733320/steam-sales-share-by-region/.

Statista (2019). Leading gaming markets worldwide 2019, by revenue (in billion US$). https://www.statista.com/statistics/308454/gaming-revenue-countries/ (Accessed January 10, 2020).

Statista (2020). Monthly number of peak concurrent players of DOTA 2 on Steam worldwide as of November 2020. https://www.statista.com/statistics/807457/ dota-2-number-players-steam/ (Accessed December 23, 2020).

Strickland, D. (2019). *Epic Store has 85 million users.* https://www.tweaktown. com/news/65310/epic-store-85-million-users/index.html. (Accessed on August 4, 2020).

Yamanaka, T. (2018). *epic gēmusu ga (Epic gēmusu sutoa) o happyō. Kaihatsu-sha ni `88-pāsento no rieki' o teikyō suru, zendaimimon no gēmu hanbai purattofōmu.* https://automaton-media.com/articles/newsjp/20181205-80879/. (Accessed on August 4, 2020).

© 2021 World Scientific Publishing Company
https://doi.org/10.1142/9789811231032_0013

Case 13

Amazon Versus Rakuten — Comparing Two Successful Business Models

Louis Chesneau

Rakuten (originally MDM Inc.) was founded by Hiroshi Mikitani in February 1997 in Japan. When created, it was the first and only e-commerce platform in the country. Today, it is still the largest e-commerce company in Japan (Saephan, 2019). However, the company wants to develop itself internationally and is facing fierce competition from other e-commerce websites like Amazon or Alibaba.

The Early Rakuten

When created, MDM Inc. was a B2B2C platform that aimed to connect individuals and companies with small regional suppliers. When Rakuten was launched, it only counted up to six employees and one server. The small online platform started by proposing the products of 13 merchants. Twenty years later, however, more than 45,000 sellers have joined the website (Rakuten Corporate Website, 2020). Back in 1997, Rakuten's project was very ambitious; indeed, it was the very beginning of the Internet era and there were only very few users then. Many people were quite skeptical about Hiroshi Mikitani's idea and told him that no one would buy anything on the Internet. More than 20 years later, we can fairly assume that he proved them wrong.

Rakuten Ichiba, which could literally be translated as "Optimism Market" in English, was launched one month after the creation of MDM Inc. It was one of the first online shopping malls. Shortly after, in 1998, "Rakuten super Auction" was created. This platform allowed MDM Inc. users to buy and sell in the auctions on the financial market. In 1999, MDM Inc. was rebranded Rakuten Inc. The company believed that using the same name for the group and its online marketplace would give more clarity to the consumer.

From the beginning, Rakuten chose to endorse a very specific strategy. Conversely, to its competitors like IBM or Amazon, Rakuten was not buying goods to resell them on its website. It was linking local merchants and customers through its online platform.

This strategy gave lots of freedom to the merchants; the latter could customize their online storefront almost entirely (WPIC, 2019). One of the drawbacks of this strategy is the lack of uniformity of the website. Moreover, during its early years, the company did not invest a lot in the design of it. This rapidly created a lack of intuitiveness on the platform, giving a considerable advantage to its competitors. Finally, the last difference with Rakuten's strategy is with the financial aspects for the merchants. Rakuten was charging them very low fees, contrary to the other e-commerce platforms. The Rakuten strategy was clear — and that was to be very appealing to the merchants in order to propose to its customers a very large catalogue of products. On the contrary, Amazon or IBM strategies were more focused on attracting the customers through a very friendly website design.

Creation of Rakuten Ecosystem

The 2000s were a key period for Rakuten; the company was rapidly growing, and it was starting to be used all over Japan. The online shopping mall was referencing 2,300 online stores and was generating almost 100 million page views per month (Dvorak, 2000). In the meantime, in order to support its strategy to give lots of freedom to its merchants, in January 2000, Rakuten inaugurated the Rakuten University. The objective of this institution was to provide knowledge about internet shop management to its merchants. This way, Rakuten was trying to make its platform consistent and optimized for consumers.

A couple of months later, in April 2000, Rakuten decided to boost its development process and went public through an IPO on the JASDAQ market. The aim was to increase brand notoriety and attract new investors that would support its future expansion projects. The company did not wait very long before making its first move. At the end of the year 2000, it redeemed one of the most famous portal sites and search engines in Japan called "Infoseek Japan K.K.".

The Rakuten Ecosystem was born. Rakuten Ecosystem could be defined as a very wide set of services, not necessarily related to each another, proposed by the group.

Once it started building its own ecosystem, Rakuten's Vision for the future was clear: to keep growing and grow fast. In 2001, CEO Hiroshi Mikatani announced the company's new objective, *reach 1 trillion Yen in terms of gross transaction value* (see Figure 1). That was a very ambitious target considering that when announced, the group was generating only 36 million gross transaction value (Rakuten Corporate Website, 2020).

In order to achieve this objective Rakuten continued to diversify its activities by proposing two new services on its website: Rakuten Travel, that offered online hotel reservation, and Rakuten Books, an online book store.

In 2002, Rakuten decided to slightly change its business model. The objective was to build a win–win relationship with its merchants. To do so, it launched the "pay as you go program". This new system combined fixed monthly fees and commissions on sales. Once again, we noticed that Rakuten really chose to emphasize in its strategy the merchants, rather than the customers. This is why a bit later, in 2002, in order to balance the strategy, the company launched the "Super Point Program".

This loyalty-based program enables consumers to get fidelity points worth 1% or 2% of their order each time they buy a product via the

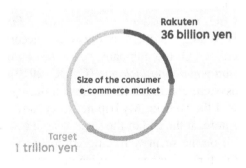

Figure 1.   Rakuten's gross transaction value in comparison with the target of 1 trillion yen (Rakuten Corporate Website, 2020).

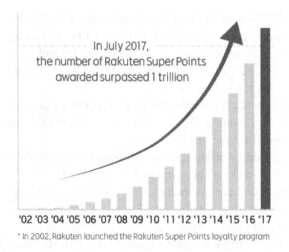

In July 2017,
the number of Rakuten Super Points
awarded surpassed 1 trillion

'02 '03 '04 '05 '06 '07 '08 '09 '10 '11 '12 '13 '14 '15 '16 '17

* In 2002, Rakuten launched the Rakuten Super Points loyalty program

Figure 2.   Total number of Rakuten super points awarded (Rakuten Corporate Website, 2020).

Rakuten website (Fauconnier, 2018). Then, they could use those points in any shop or for any service available on Rakuten's platform (see Figure 2).

Nowadays, such programs are very common, but back in 2002, for an e-commerce platform, it was really ahead of its time. A year later, Rakuten reinforced this strategy by creating the "Rakuten Point Club", allowing its users to enjoy special discount offers depending on the number of points they have accumulated. Rakuten was the first e-commerce platform to conduct such a practice, which gave it a significant advantage over its competitors in Japan. Realizing this, the company invested a lot to support the strategy. Over the years, it offered more than 1 billion "Super Points" to the club members, which, according to Fabien Versavau, the French Rakuten entity CEO, *represents around 10 million Euros* (Fauconnier, 2018). And, this strategy worked really well; according to Hiroshi Mikitani, Rakuten's CEO, the company has a *100-million membership, out of a 130-million population in Japan* (CNBC, 2019).

Rakuten Ecosystem continued its expansion during 2003. The company fully acquired the website MyTrip.net to enhance its online travel business. Furthermore, at the end of the same year, it acquired DLJ Direct SFG securities, an online security trading company. This company was the first to offer this type of financial service in Japan and was the seventh largest online brokerage in the United States during the 2000s (Hanabusa, 1999). For Rakuten, it represented a very important investment, but it was

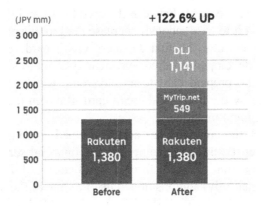

Figure 3.   Rakuten's net profit growth after M&As (Rakuten Corporate Website, 2020).

in line with its ambitious objective of reaching the trillion yen online transaction value.

After its M&A operations, we can see on the graph that Rakuten almost tripled its original net profit and experienced a growth of more than 120% to reach 3,000 million Yen (see Figure 3) (Rakuten Corporate Website, 2020).

Strengthening a unique business model:

In 2004, Rakuten continued diversifying its business activity; this time, the company decided to invest in the sports sphere. To do so, it created the Rakuten Baseball Inc. This entity quickly acquired the Sendai Baseball team and turned it into a professional team, the Tohoku Rakuten Golden Eagles. As baseball is the most popular sport in Japan, for Rakuten, this operation represented a massive boost in communication, especially since in the first year, the team achieved victory. That made them the first new professional team to win in over 50 years. It instantly spread the brand nationwide.

In the meantime, the group continued developing its ecosystem through more M&A operations. For instance, it fully acquired an online community of job seekers Minnano Shushoku Inc. and also Azora Card Co. Ltd., a company that provides credit cards. Rakuten's ecosystem entered then, for the first time, into the online banking sector. The company strongly believed that the credit card business was a great way to increase its profit, and it was right. After acquiring Azora, Rakuten redeemed another credit card dealer, Kokunai Shinpan Co. Ltd. And then, it finally launched its own credit card payment service known as

Rakuten Card. The synergy between the credit card and the e-commerce services enabled it to tremendously increase the group's profit. Indeed, in 2018, Rakuten became the first Japanese credit card retailer (Mitobe, 2018) and has developed different payment systems to suit all Japanese people. From the prepaid card to an electronic wallet called "Rakuten Pay", swinging by the traditional credit card, Rakuten manages to cover all types of payment methods.

Since 2008, the company has also developed its banking system by creating Rakuten Bank Ltd. Feeling that the financial service sector has huge growth potential, Rakuten formed an alliance with Bit Wallet (now known as Rakuten Edy) and positioned itself as one of the pioneers in the e-money business. As mentioned by Tatsuya Kubo, Rakuten's Card director in 2018, the company is *number one in terms of transaction number in Japan and the financial activity is expected to double up this year* (Fauconnier, 2018). This statement confirms that the idea to invest in the online banking sector so early had paid off.

Another sector aspiring to become one of the most important for the Rakuten ecosystem is telecommunications. In 2007, the group made its first steps in the telephony business by acquiring the company Fusion Communication Corp. A bit more than 10 years after this acquisition, the company would become the first mobile operator of Japan. It now counts more than 1.5 million subscribers and 200 stores all over the country (Fauconnier, 2018).

As we can see in Figure 4, Rakuten is now involved in 10 different sectors, and its almost classic company model is very representative of the Japanese company expansion style. Conversely to an American or European-based company, instead of staying in a chosen field, it tried to diversify its activity as much as possible. This way, the company can mitigate the risk linked to each business.

Managing such a business is not easy and that is why in 2006, Rakuten introduced the "growth management program".

Through this program, Rakuten restructured its organization and divided it into 38 business units. This way, it was easier for each business unit to manage its own profitability and growth. As the group was constantly growing, it needed regular restructuration. In 2008, Rakuten had 40 different businesses and services. In order to enhance investment efficiency and compare financial results more easily, the company regrouped the business units into 11 business groups (Rakuten Corporate Website, 2020). In the same way, to manage such a big company, human resources

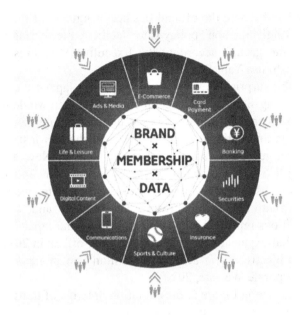

Figure 4.   Concept of the Rakuten ecosystem (Rakuten Corporate Website, 2020).

started to become an essential stack. That is why during the year 2007, it invested a lot of money in that department and decided to move the head-quarters to the Shinagawa seaside, in the Rakuten Tower in Tokyo. The company believed that this work environment was nicer for the employees and might lead to a greater outcome for the company.

Global expansion strategy

Back in 2005, Rakuten took its first step overseas by acquiring a US-based marketing company called LinkShare Corporation. This com-pany would later be renamed Rakuten Marketing LLC.

In 2008, in order to boost its revenue, Rakuten decided to establish its first foreign shopping mall. By establishing a joint venture with a leading retail company in Taiwan, "President Chain Store Corp", Rakuten launched its online shopping mall abroad.

Then, 2010 was been a key year for Rakuten. Its status changed from a large domestic company to a multinational corporation. In order to ease that transition, Rakuten started the "Englishization" of the company.

Hence, English became the official business language of the group. The goal of the "Englishization" policy is to "facilitate the sharing of information among the group" according the Executive Vice President of the company, Yoshihisa Yamada (CNN, 2017).

It was a bit surprising at first, especially for a Japanese company, but that gave a strong signal to all its competitors. Rakuten would not limit its expansion to Japan as it wanted to become the e-commerce world leader. To increase its international presence, it established an institute of technology in charge of Research and Development in New York. It also acquired the US-based e-commerce website Buy.com and the French e-commerce website Price Minister. Those two websites were important e-commerce platforms in their respective countries and, consequently, those acquisitions represent a lot of strength from the Japanese brand.

This global expansion strategy quickly paid off, as in 2011, it finally reached its objective — it achieved a trillion yen in transaction value (Rakuten Corporate Website, 2020).

As we can see in Figure 5, the evolution in terms of transaction value was almost exponential from 2000 to 2011.

Reaching the trillion yen in gross transaction value took the company 10 years and 38,000 merchants on the platform. That is an incredible growth from the 2500 merchants it had when the trillion objective was defined (Rakuten Corporate Website, 2020).

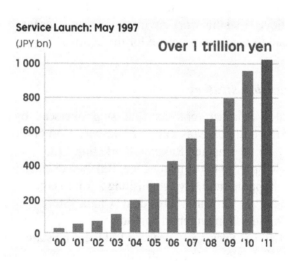

Figure 5.   Rakuten Ichiba gross transaction value (Rakuten Corporate Website, 2020).

Over the year 2011, Rakuten continued its globalization; after a US and a French e-commerce website, the Japanese company bought "Ikeda internet Software", a Brazilian e-commerce platform, and "Tradoria GMBH", a German one. A year later, the Japanese group also acquired the Spanish video platform "Wuaki.tv" and the Canadian e-book company "Kobo Inc". At the time, "Kobo Inc." was one of the leaders of the e-reading sector. This sector would become one of the principal areas of development for Rakuten over the years. The company truly believed that online books would quickly replace printed books. Hence, in 2015, Rakuten fully acquired "OverDrive Holdings", Inc., a leading e-book content provider primarily for libraries. And, in 2018, Rakuten partnered with Walmart to become one of the leaders in the e-book market (Corkery, 2018).

In order to fully enter the American e-commerce market, Rakuten bought the online cash-back website "Ebates". This other foot on US soil helped the Japanese company compete against its major rivals Amazon and Alibaba.

As a result, Rakuten is now present in eight different countries as an e-commerce platform or other service provider and is also involved in more business fields than ever.

The Nippon company keeps investing in R&D through the development of institutes of technology all across the world. After Tokyo and New York, Rakuten established three new research centers: one in Paris, one in Singapore and one in Boston.

But, even if Rakuten is present in several countries, the company understood the importance of keeping the businesses separate and adapted the management style to each country. *For the Ecosystem to grow, each business needs to flourish, that's the foundation of our force,* ensured Toshihiko Otsuka, the Rakuten Europe Director (Fauconnier, 2018).

A Company That Keeps Evolving

In 2013, Rakuten public shares were upgraded from the JASDAQ (the standard market) to the first section on the Tokyo stock exchange index (TOPIX), a section reserved for very large companies. But, Rakuten is always looking for more and continues to develop the sectors it believes are the most promising. The first was the telecommunications sector. Rakuten fully acquired Viber, one of the main competitors of WhatsApp in the messaging app industry. This acquisition enabled Rakuten to enter

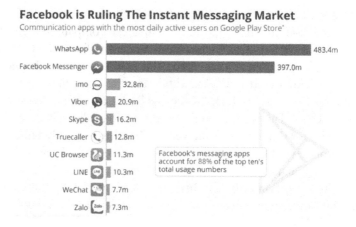

Figure 6.   Free messaging app daily users in 2018 (Wagner, 2018).

both the paying and free telecommunications market. With the explosion of the Internet, entering the free app messaging market was mandatory for Rakuten in order to maintain its leadership position on the global telecommunication market. Rakuten plans to develop Viber and make it a more complete app. It wants it to become *the Japanese WeChat* (Fauconnier, 2018).

Since its acquisition in 2014, Viber users have only been increasing (Clement, 2019). With 20.9 million daily users in 2018, Viber has great potential for growth (see Figure 6) (Wagner, 2019).

The second sector Rakuten continued to develop was e-commerce with the launch of "Rakuma". It is an application where non-professionals could buy and sell items from each other. Hence, you do not need to be a professional merchant anymore to sell your product and make money on Rakuten. This opened the range of possible transactions for the Japanese company.

The corporation also understood that making the online purchasing experience closer to the physical purchasing experience would enable it to reach a wider target market. Indeed, one of the drawbacks of online shopping is that you cannot physically try the product. To overcome this problem, the Nippon firm acquired the company "fits.me", which provides a virtual experience of a fitting room to the customers. This way, Rakuten consumers are able to try on the product they intend to buy. All those improvements on its e-commerce platform also enabled Rakuten to differentiate itself from its competitors as none of its direct rivals were proposing such services.

The ecosystem advantages

Rakuten started to rely on digital data to address consumers with more customized offers. That is why in 2014, it bought Slice, a company that sells intelligence based on digital commerce measurement. Indeed, this company analyzes the consumers' purchasing history through the emails they receive from the major e-commerce websites. But, this is not completely new for Rakuten. Conversely to its competitors, its network enables the Japanese company to target its consumers easily. For example, Rakuten Card users provide the company information on their transactions which can then be used by Rakuten to make a customized suggestion of product on its website. Equally, if someone buys a trip on Rakuten Travel and then goes to the e-book website, this person will be offered trip guides for the purchased destination. Tracking consumer behavior and targeting is not very recent, but this new tool allows Rakuten to have access to the transactions made by its competitors as well. Data gathering has become one of the major marketing tools for e-commerce platforms, but it is not the only one that Rakuten uses.

Brand Management

The end of the year 2013 had been great for Rakuten; its baseball team the Tohoku Rakuten Golden Eagles won the Major Professional Japanese baseball league. It gave them a huge boost of notoriety and global appreciation from the Japanese people.

After the success with the acquisition of a baseball team, Rakuten kept investing in sports. In 2015, it fully acquired the professional football club Vissel Kobe, a team which is part of the Japanese major football league, the J1 League.

However, the objective for Rakuten was clear; it needed to increase its notoriety overseas. To do so, at the end of 2016, it launched its biggest marketing operation. Indeed, it officially announced that the Brand would become FC Barcelona's main sponsor (Marsden, 2016). FC Barcelona is one of the most symbolic and well-known football clubs in Europe. Rakuten's name will appear on the jersey of each Barcelona player for

Figure 7. FC Barcelona sponsorship with Rakuten campaign (Rakuten Corporate Website, 2020).

every game during the 2017–2018 season (see Figure 7). This massive deal represented 220 million euros. The next year, Rakuten also became the official sponsor of the Golden State Warriors, one of the best teams in the American Major Basketball league (NBA). At the time, the Golden State Warriors had won the basketball league two times over the previous three years. With some iconic players like Stephen Curry and Kevin Durant, doing a partnership with this team would drastically increase Rakuten's notoriety in the US. Finally, Rakuten recently became the first foreign company to own a Chinese professional baseball league team. It acquired the Lamigo Monkeys and renamed it the Rakuten Monkeys, with jerseys designed similarly to the Tohoku Rakuten Golden Eagles. According to Rahul Kadavakolu, executive branding and sponsoring director of the group, thanks to those partnerships, Rakuten's *"notoriety has skyrocketed, especially as Facebook, Google, or Amazon were not present in the sports sponsoring, it enabled us to differentiate"* (Fauconnier, 2019).

Competition and Major Challenges

Because Rakuten's network is incredibly large, *comparing Rakuten Ichiba with Amazon and other competitors is not relevant, we need to compare the ecosystem, says* Naho Kono, president of the e-commerce group (Fauconnier, 2019).

According to Kono, *as a whole Rakuten ecosystem is currently more profitable than Amazon's, especially after all they invest to develop*

MALGRÉ UN HAUT NIVEAU D'ACTIVITÉ, UNE CAPITALISATION TRÈS BASSE			
	Volume global de transactions 2017 (Mrds$)	Capitalisation boursière au 31 mai 2018 (Mrds$)	Marge opérationnelle 2017
Alibaba	768*	507,1	28%
Amazon	350**	790,7	2%
JD	200	50,5	0%
Rakuten	115	9,8	17%
eBay	88	37,5	24%
Mercadolibre	12	12,8	9%

Figure 8. Operational figures of the main e-market competitors, Libre Service Actualité estimations (Fauconnier, 2018).

amazon prime (Fauconnier, 2019). That being said, in terms of transaction value, and even more in market capitalization, Rakuten is far behind its competitors as we can see in Figure 8.

This very low market capitalization is explained by the fact that Rakuten's network is tremendously large and is very complicated to understand for the investors. As it is involved in more businesses than its competitors and has deviated from its original business, Rakuten's valuation will tend to be underestimated compared to its direct rivals.

What is interesting is that Rakuten does not see the future of e-commerce the same way the two giant leaders Amazon and Alibaba do. Instead of converting itself into a retailer, Rakuten positioned itself as a partner that would help the traditional distributor to embrace the future. The company has strong social values due to its Japanese heritage of the Shinto culture. This way of doing business surely differentiates it from its competitors; nevertheless, we will see in the future if it can suit every marketplace around the world.

The major axis that Rakuten is currently thinking about developing is logistics.

Rakuten does not have its own delivery service and, consequently, this is reflected in higher shipping prices and longer delivery times than its competitors. Indeed, in order to compete with the two market leaders that have already distinguished themselves by their incredibly sharp logistics, Rakuten plans to open several warehouses in Europe. *In the short term, we absolutely need infrastructure in Europe, operated by our group or a contractor,* states Fabien Versavau (Fauconnier, 2018). In the near future, logistic improvement will be a major challenge for Rakuten.

A second axis Rakuten will need to improve is the design of its website. It needs to become way more intuitive and attractive if the Nippon brand wants to catch up to its American and Chinese competitors.

Questions

1. Identify Rakuten's development strategy.
2. How does this strategy differ from a usual Western company's development strategy?
3. What are Rakuten's strengths and weaknesses compared to its competitors? And, can e-commerce-only websites be considered as competitors?
4. What would you recommend to Rakuten in order to continue its expansion?

References

Clement, J. (2020). Viber: number of registered user IDs 2011-2020. https://www.statista.com/statistics/316414/viber-messenger-registered-users/.

CNBC (2019). Rakuten vs. Amazon: The battle for Japan's e-commerce market. https://www.cnbc.com/video/2019/04/29/rakuten-vs-amazon-the-battle-for-japans-e-commerce-market.html.

CNN (2017). Go inside the 'Amazon of Japan'- https://money.cnn.com/video/technology/2017/03/29/rakuten-made-in-japan.cnnmoney/index.html.

Corkery, M. (2018). Walmart Makes a Late Entry Into the E-Book Market. https://www.nytimes.com/2018/01/25/business/walmart-ebooks-kobo-japan.html.

Dvorak, P. (2000). Japan's Highly Popular Rakuten Plans IPO Despite Shaky Market. https://www.wsj.com/articles/SB95599758475089432.

Fauconnier, F. (2018). Rakuten, l'autre géant de l'e-commerce, Flore Fauconnier. https://www.lsa-conso.fr/rakuten-l-autre-geant-de-l-e-commerce,289996.

Hanabusa, M. (1999). DLJdirect is First Foreign Company Selling Online Trading in Japan. https://www.totaltele.com/427204/DLJdirect-is-First-Foreign-Company-Selling-Online-Trading-in-Japan.

Marsden, S. (2016). Barcelona agree four-year short sponsorship deal with Rakuten. https://global.espn.com/football/barcelona/story/2997556/barcelona-agree-four-year-shirt-sponsorship-deal-with-rakuten.

Mitobe, T. (2018). Rakuten takes the lead in Japan's credit card market. https://asia.nikkei.com/Business/Companies/Rakuten-takes-the-lead-in-Japan-s-credit-card-market.

Rakuten Corporate Website (2020). https://www.rakuten.com/ Accessed on November 12, 2020.

Wagner, P. (2018). Facebook is Ruling the Instant Messaging Market. https://www.statista.com/chart/13711/top-10-instant-messaging-apps-on-android/.

WPIC (2019). The Battle for Japan: The future of Rakuten and Amazon.jp. Accessed December 24, 2020. https://www.wpic.co/blog/the-battle-for-japan-the-future-of-rakuten-and-amazon-jp/.

© 2021 World Scientific Publishing Company
https://doi.org/10.1142/9789811231032_bmatter

Index

Printed in the United States
by Baker & Taylor Publisher Services